Reincarnation Through Common Sense

by Doug "Ten" Rose

To Dennis,
Not many left that Know for almost
as long as I Know myself. Very glad you
are! Stay well & stay long,
Love
Doug

Further information regarding the project for sponsoring wisdom professionals, the author, *The Dog Soldier Trilogy*, or whatever else we can help you with is available upon your request by contacting:

Fearless Puppy Publishing
ten@fearlesspuppy.org

Or see our website at:
http://www.fearlesspuppy.org

ISBN 978-0692019528

Also by Doug "Ten" Rose
Fearless Puppy on American Road, 2013

Edit, layout, and design
Alathea Windsong Daniels
windsong@mtnhome.com

*"All my life I have tried
to pluck a thistle
and plant a flower
wherever the flower would grow
in thought and mind."*

Abraham Lincoln

*"The Constitution only guarantees people
the right to the pursuit of happiness.
You have to catch it yourself."*

Ben Franklin

*"The most revolutionary act
a person can perform in this country
is to be happy."*

Dr. Patch Adams

&

Reincarnation Through Common Sense
Table of Contents

The Sing Along Section

Reincarnation

Final Scenes

ᕫ

Glossary

Almost all of the words in *Reincarnation Through Common Sense* are in English. Once in a while, the use of the local language here in Southeast Asia could not be avoided. Language, and even more so the lack of language, is certainly a big part of this story. Here are a few non-English words that will rarely, if ever, pop up.

Wat = Temple
bai nai = Where are you going? What's up?
chai = true, or yes, or brother
Farang = Caucasian foreigner/alien
korp koon (kahp/kah*) = thank you
kor thot (kahp/kah*) = excuse me
mahk = much
mai = not
mai chai = no, or false
mai kow jai = I don't understand
Phra = Monk
Phram = Monk student, novice, or assistant

Sa wat dee (kahp/kah*) = Hello, goodbye, and several other meanings

*A male speaker uses the word *kahp* at the end of almost every phrase. A female speaker uses the word *kah*. These are the most commonly used words in the language. The literal translation is, "As the man/woman I am, *I respect you*."

Acknowledgments

There are so many people to thank that it would fill an entire book to do it correctly. To those whom space won't allow me to mention, I apologize and thank you deeply. You know who you are.

Big Paul Hickman of Manchester, England is a trainer and equipment manufacturer for Asian boxers. He is an extraordinary human being who helped me to stay alive for long enough to start this story.

The Ortiz family, the Blomberg Jr. family, the Fort family, and Mr. Bryan P. Ayers embody generosity, friendship, and faith in humanity. Their sacrificial actions on behalf of nearly everything they come into contact with demonstrate what's good about people.

The entire Cornell University community has shown compassion and given assistance above and beyond the call of duty. The higher ups may be nice too, but I'm talking about the students and working staff. I was destitute, homeless, and injured when we met. Although I was never a student there, the Cornell folks treated me better than I treated myself. They taught me how to use a computer.

The mother of these books is Alathea Windsong Daniels, who for a long time served as managing editor of the Cherokee-based Good Medicine Society publication *The Flowering Tree.* We've traded several thousand emails and spent several thousand hours together—on the Internet. Alathea is bashful, and is probably smart to be so. If she weren't reclusive, guys would be hovering around her like bees at a honeycomb. Windsong is the most diligent, patient, focused, strong, in-touch-with-it, and warmhearted woman I have never met.

This book could not have been written without the kindness, generosity, patience, and talent of Nancy Crompton.

The late, great Joann Benjamin Kaplan and the vivacious Mary Lauderdale Hart were both kind enough to put up with me for several of my craziest years. That was forty years ago. They have given valuable contributions to this book much more recently.

Great thanks to David Arndt and Elizabeth at the Drikung Dharma Center of Lincoln, Vermont, and to Eileen/Michael/CJ/Tammy and everyone at the RigDzin Dharma Center of Albuquerque, New Mexico. CJ Ondek has one of the biggest brainhearts on Earth and editing eyes as well.

Lama Traga Rinpoche, H.E. Garchen Rinpoche, Gape Lama, Lama Abo, Lama Bunima, Lama Sonam, Lama Pema, Lama Drupon Rinchen Dorje, Lama Gursam, Lama Rebkong, Lama Rangbar, Lama Ontul Rinpoche, and Tashe Dolma have had a huge positive influence on many folks. I am one. Many thanks also to Lama Karma Rinchen, the KJML community, and to all my friends in Truth or Consequences, New Mexico.

Speaking of friends and teachers, I have had the incredible luck to know some folks who are both at the same time. None have been more brilliant and kind than H.H. Seonaidh John Perks and The Venerable Julia Perks of Celtic Buddhism. They have each lent me brain cells when my supply was dwindling. They are awesome examples of what the saintly can do with their lives while still remaining approachable and unpretentious human beings.

The greater Brattleboro, Vermont community and everybody in it just plain rocks! They embody what it should feel like in a comparatively sane and certainly progressive small city. It has been a great privilege for me to live in Brattleboro, and a great benefit to be surrounded by its residents.

Beth Ann Ortiz introduced me to that community. We don't come from the same parents, but no man ever had a better sister. She is at once a rock that stabilizes, a mother that nurtures, a fire that inspires and warms, and a devout practitioner of decency and honor. On the other hand, don't fuck with her or she'll chew you up and spit out the shreds.

The diligent proofreading efforts and friendships of Lise LePage (and Chris Grotke) of www.iBrattleboro.com have been a great help in making this book readable. Many thanks also to the insightful literary minds and kindness of Leslie Jacob Sommers and Cheryl Ray. My gratitude also goes out to the generous efforts of Glen Gill, Debra and Cody Oakland, Lindsay Cobb, and Susan Sanborn.

Last, and the exact opposite of least, my literally undying gratitude goes out to anyone whose main concern is the well being of all living creatures as a whole—and especially to those people who have mustered the strength, courage, and invested the energy to do something constructive with that concern. Sure, there are a few like the Dalai Lama and Mother Teresa who always come to mind first, but there are much less famous examples to be seen every day. More folks than you might imagine have a concern-for-us-all. These are the people who remind us that we don't have to be slaves to bullshit—not our own or anyone else's.

Dedication

Our beautiful planet is decaying rapidly.

Chronic fears dissolve cooperation and cripple joy.
Human decency suffers inhumane abuse.
We are a wounded species.

What went wrong? Who is to blame?

It doesn't matter.
The only things that matter now are the things that will help.

We are an intelligent species
with the potential for great compassion and accomplishment.
We are able to fix what has gone wrong.

This book is dedicated to our only hope.

This book is dedicated to you.

The Beginning

"The greatest thing a human soul ever does in this world is to see something and tell what it saw in a plain way. Hundreds of people can talk for one who can think, but thousands can think for one who can see. To see clearly is poetry, prophecy, and religion all rolled into one."

John Ruskin

1

Introduction * Essential Information

You'll love this book. If you don't think much of it, complain to yourself. You had as much to do with it as I did. You saved my life and then helped me to write about it. Before the story begins, I want to thank you for that.

These strange but true statements will be explained in a minute. You might as well get used to the "strange, but true" thing quickly. It will appear often.

Reincarnation Through Common Sense tells two inseparable stories—a firsthand account of one person bravely trying to become less of a jackass and a secondhand account of the Wisdom Professionals who made his effort possible. This book was written in the Buddhist Temple that I have been living in for the past several months. My fellow residents, the Monks and Nuns, are Wisdom Professionals. Their job description is to get smarter, be kinder, and help as many living creatures as they can.

The purpose of nearly all spiritual disciplines is to help us become better people. Buddhism is no exception. "Don't be a jackass" could be considered the cardinal rule. The Monks and Nuns here take that basic sentiment to some very great lengths. Most of *Reincarnation Through Common Sense* describes the positive effects that wise and compassionate influences can have on mental and physical health. There is very little mention of sex, drugs, or rock and roll in this book (especially as compared with the raw accounts in Book 1 of this trilogy, *Fearless Puppy on American Road*). There is a lot of happiness in this book. A Monastery/Nunnery can house a lot more fun and excitement than most folks would imagine.

This tale, on the surface, is a cheery and adventurous byproduct of suicidal psychosis bundled with some valuable information from previous experiences and surrounded by a shield of compassion. But if you pay attention, you will find more in this book than can be seen on the surface. There are scientific methods of alleviating mental suffering beneath that surface, and explanations of how these processes can improve your health and happiness.

This book is fun. It is about an impressive, sometimes comical comeback from near fatal mental decay and misadventure.

Section Two is the exception to the "fun" thing. One of the symptoms of a mind being sick is that it doesn't know it is. That fact is very obvious in Section Two. I thought about picking up the whole snarling thing and moving it to the end of the book where it could do less harm—but I was afraid it might beat the shit out of an Appendix or two after beating itself nearly to death. Do yourself a favor. Skip it and start reading again at Section Three. From there on, most of the book relates a more enjoyable experience. I think the Master Teacher would like that. You might too. But if you like drama, pathos, venom, and both sides of the story right up front, the unabridged version including Section Two is for you. It contains the fire that singes anyone trying to rise above the flames. The rest of the book is about the rising above part.

Several people have told me that they would like more detail of the personal disasters. Sorry, I won't do it. There are two reasons.

First of all, there's not much to tell. I was born on the edge of sanity and until my recent stay at this Temple, I lived there. There was never a need for excessive trauma or drama to push me over the edge. I made that trip several times, decades before this book was even a twinkle in the Buddha's eye. In addition to congenital insanity, six months of being drunk twenty four hours a day didn't help either. That can make you want to kill yourself even if you started out perfectly sane!

The second reason for not going into detail of personal problems is more important than the first. It doesn't seem right to ask you to spend money and time on a book that makes you feel worse. It also feels wrong for me to have to rehash old traumas and bullshit that might make me feel worse. The dead will bury the dead. I've found it better to forgive and forget—others and myself—than to give bygone traumas any extra chances to mess with me. Why dwell on what went wrong? Many people live in relationships based on sharing wounds and mutual misery. I'd rather not. Neither would most folks, if they thought about it for a minute. That's why you'll find Section Two very much shorter than the other chapters and there will be very little mention of personal problems anywhere else.

I'm generally as lucky as a monkey on a banana boat. I'm grateful for that, even though so many years were spent on stormy seas. It seems ridiculous to annoy myself and everyone else by whining about a few waves, no matter how big they were. The only reason *any* trauma has been included at all is to keep the story honest and to set the stage for all the good stuff that follows.

You'll notice that throughout most of the book I avoid using the real name of the country that this true story takes place in. There is good reason for this. When this writing began, I was bitter, bent, and looking for someone or something else to blame—as many folks do when their life hits the fan. Everything was my scapegoat, including this country and its people.

But no matter how much we try to deny responsibility for our own difficulties, the truth will eventually govern. When I finally grew sane enough to find my own ass, it became obvious that my head was up it. As the old expression says, "No matter where you go, there you are." My problems were, for the most part, caused by me. The country they happened in holds no particular fault and should not be considered in a bad light. Let's call this country by the fictional name of *Honoria* as a sign of respect for it, and as my apology to it.

I spoke no Honorian upon arrival at the Temple and still know very little. It is a very different and difficult language for a Westerner to learn. The Monks and Nuns at this Temple communicate a comforting glow by simply being present, but none of them speak English. Our Head Monk speaks some English, but he travels a lot. When home with us, he is always busy. Villagers and clergy alike constantly seek his counsel. My other Temple mates speak no English at all. Regular verbal communication was never an option. Hand, sign, and body language are the main methods. This nonverbal "speech" has often accomplished more clarity of communication than any attempts at verbal conversation could. At times it has accomplished more clarity of communication than my conversations with fellow English speakers!

Writing *Reincarnation Through Common Sense* has been a severely mad challenge. Speaking about silence isn't easy. Just describing the very foreign living experience, much less relaying the wordless philosophical concepts that this living experience is based on, might scare even the best of professional writers. Luckily, I'm not a professional writer. I'm a guy from Brooklyn trying to tell his friends about a very unusual, almost otherworldly experience. As a conversation with friends, this book has been fun to write, and I think it will be fun for you to read. Had I tried to stay within the regularly accepted norms and forms of English literature, I'd have probably lost my mind again and started to eat the bar napkins and paper towels that most of this book was first written on.

Ninety percent of *Reincarnation Through Common Sense* is true. The other ten percent is also true, but perhaps only through the filter of my own eyes. What you'll read are my personal and very subjective perceptions. Many are interpretations of the silence so prevalent at the Temple. Anyone confusing subjective and objective reality is in big trouble. I was in big trouble, but still managed to separate the ramblings of my warped mind from the realities of what was going on in the world around me most of the time, but not all of the time. My accounts will give accurate descriptions and insights, but won't interfere with the vision each reader will bring to, and get from, this story. I may pull a bus up to your front door, but you'll be writing your own ticket.

Except for the quotes, this is all the work of one author. But it doesn't feel as if I actually wrote all of the material you will read. There are things in this book that are smarter than I am. My Temple family has, at least indirectly, been responsible for anything that resembles wisdom within these pages. Psychospiritual processes constantly surround the Monks and Nuns. Small bits of these processes seem to have rubbed off on me through no real effort of my own. It seems as if some of the material in this book floated into my brain from the Monks and Nuns and I've just been transferring it into English words.

Really, folks. No joke. I was nuts while the earliest writing was being done but am quite sane now and still believe this to be true. The Temple residents haven't *done* anything to me. They were never concerned that I write anything at all, much less anything specific. No spell was cast, no thought form or hocus pocus induced, and not a single literary suggestion was ever offered. Nonetheless, simply by them being who they are and my being around them, the Temple people had a lot to do with the better and kinder interpretations within this story.

The writing styles bounce around almost as much as the author's brain did. There is a lot of prose, bits of poetry, and some almost hip hop/ rap style internal rhyme pieces. Some folks will think nothing of these style changes. To others, these shifts may seem out of sync and even weird—at first. But by the time Section Three ends, the logic of Albert Einstein's very Buddhist statement should be obvious to everyone.

*"Once you accept the universe as being something
expanding into an infinite nothing which is something,
wearing stripes with plaid is easy."*

Albert Einstein

For the most part, everything is presented in the order that it was written. The exception is The Sing Along Section, which was among the first material written but is now Section Four. This collection of bizarre fun in tune form was originally sold to the very few tourists who visited the Temple. It made some of them dizzy and nauseated. Others thought it brilliant. The price I charged for the collection was two packs of cigarettes. Most of the folks who read it told me it was worth at least three.

The word "Arjan" translates from the native language to English as "teacher." It is also an honorific title used when speaking to or about the Head Monk of any Temple. Arjan Dang is the name of the Head Monk/ Master Teacher at my Temple of residence. When he found out I was writing, he said, "Oh good! Writing a book for Westerners in English about life in an Asian Temple. Very good!" He didn't know exactly what was being written and still has no idea about Section Two!

Becoming an author was never on my to-do list. These books are only being produced as a vehicle to fund the education of Monks, Nuns, Shamans, Medicine Men and Women, and other Wisdom Professionals. All author profits from these books will be donated to that cause. Anyone who makes a life's work of promoting emotional intelligence over habitual ignorance deserves assistance. The type of intelligent stability and compassion that these Wisdom Professionals are capable of awakening in folks is desperately needed right now. If you don't believe me, read a newspaper. For more explanation about the project to fund Wisdom Professionals, see Appendix 2, *Why the Dog Soldier Trilogy Is Being Written.*

2

The Story

"The universe is made up of stories, not atoms."

Muriel Rukeyser

This Temple is a very spiritual place. No one knows exactly what "spirit" is, although everyone seems to know that they have it. Many people keep unknown quantities such as spirit on the fringe of their lives. They figure that if they can't see, smell, taste, hear, have sex with, or spend something, it doesn't deserve much attention. Other folks build their whole lives around this unknown quantity called spirit without ever developing a concrete definition of it. This may be a lot saner than it sounds.

I think of myself as a somewhat spiritual person, but that isn't what landed me in this Temple or why the folks in robes continue to let me stay. I was a psychotic suicidal alcoholic stranded in a very foreign country with no knowledge of its language, no money, and no ability to make sense to myself or anyone else.

The Monks and Nuns here work diligently at perfecting wisdom and kindness. They are unshakably dedicated to it, and very good at putting that kindness and wisdom into action.

These people have adopted me. Like only the luckiest of unwanted puppies about to be destroyed at the pound, I was rescued at the eleventh hour. By decree of their Master Teacher (whose word is the law here), the Monks are now my brothers and the Nuns are my sisters. I don't have to study any Buddhism, do any work in this place, or search for survival money elsewhere. I was told, "Feel like you are at home with good family."

Let's get something straight right from the beginning. I am no smarter or more special than anyone reading this. I think you probably could have handled much of this experience at least as well as I did. Luck landed me in the right place, at the right time, and surrounded me with the right people. Dumb ass good luck and realizing that bullshit is temporary are the main things responsible for my now being alive, happy, and a lot smarter than just a few months ago.

That "bullshit is only temporary" thing comes in *very* handy.

After fifty years of living and a lot of research, Honoria sounded like the best place to start a new life. I had very little money by American standards and had previously never been overseas, unless a trip from Brooklyn to New Jersey counts.

I drank too much alcohol for several months following my arrival in Asia and married too quickly. I was then used and abused by my own bad judgment and drunken stupidity. My wife and others took advantage of my dull mind and relative wealth ($9,000 total). I lost everything—the money, woman, home, small business, and the desire to deal with life. Anger at the world, and especially at myself, grew to the point of insanity.

After discreetly buying narcotic pills in small doses over a week's time, there were enough on hand to finish me. I'd made several friends during the previous year. They started to coincidentally show up at just the wrong times for me to complete my escape from Earth. It was incredible how every time my resolve was bucked up enough to grab those pills, there was a knock on the door. My friends still have no idea how often they prevented my end.

These friends came to Honoria from many different countries. Expatriates often get close to each other quickly. These same folks, in the security of their home country, might not have become so rapidly concerned about a stranger. Luckily for me, bonds had been forged. (A few Honorian nationals were involved as well.)

One of these friends was a German national named Sepp who was fluent in the local language. He knocked on my door one morning with his standard singularly worded greeting, "Beer!" We shared several beers before Sepp stood up to say, "Come with me please. You belong in the Temple." He drove us the twenty miles to the Temple and translated a conversation between Arjan and myself. By the end of that conversation I asked Arjan, who as Head Monk makes all such decisions, for permission to stay a while.

Mine was not a normal type of decision. There was no think, weigh options, then decide. It felt more like the decision made me than it felt like I made the decision! It was as if my trauma was lightened by Arjan's simply being who he was, and by my being in the same room with him. I wouldn't have walked out of that place any sooner than a plant would turn its back on the sun.

Arjan's job description is to be a benevolent presence, a metaphorical human sun that people can turn to for helpful energy. He told me to not worry about the Buddhism part of Temple life—or anything else. Arjan advised me to just relax and make myself comfortable. He welcomed me to take part in Temple activities or to just swim at the beach and lounge around the grounds. Whatever I wanted to do, or not do, was fine with him.

"Make yourself comfortable" is the theme behind everything Arjan has ever told me. This phrase contains an intense and immense amount more power than it initially seems to contain. I didn't understand how much more, until Arjan showed me the deeper meaning. The concept behind this phrase has bailed me out of hell many times. Arjan's deeper interpretation of "Make yourself comfortable" is explained later in this book.

Arjan said to treat him, the Monks, Nuns, and the hundred or so neighboring villagers like brothers, sisters, and friends. He called himself the older brother of my new family. He did not ask then, nor has he asked since, for anything in return—not a dime, not a prayer, not a promise.

The words "teacher" and "student" have never been used in our conversations, but the student/teacher process began at that first meeting and has deepened ever since.

Sometimes, just when you think it will never happen again, you can get very, very lucky. I will always be grateful to the villagers, the Monks and Nuns who adopted me, and to you. After all, my friend, even though we never actually met, I did decide to write to you instead of killing myself. When I needed someone to talk with most, no one spoke my language. *Any* conversation was impossible without you. If not for you, the crippling loneliness of not being able to speak or listen may have combined with the mind shattering strangeness of the environment and the sadness of my circumstance. That would have been the perfect mental storm, and likely fatal to me.

I knew that someday you would be reading this. My being psychotic at the time doesn't change the facts. Your influence on me was very real. You saved my life as surely as anyone else mentioned in these pages.

Thank you.

P.S. A friend recently went to a meditation center and then came to me disappointed. He said the people there didn't meet up to his expectations. He expected calm compassion to be oozing from them, and that each would have a Dalai Lama-like demeanor. But most were just regular folks, some were very pleasant, and one was downright ornery. My friend said, "These people are supposed to be better than that!"

I asked him if everyone in his church acted like Jesus or Mother Teresa. He understood.

Calm compassion, a lot of rage against the machine, a small bit of depression, a lot of joy, and some comedy are within this story. In varying percentages, we are each made up of those elements. Evolution keeps happening. We continually work on increasing the more positive and pleasant, while decreasing the causes of suffering. No matter how smart we may already be, we never stop growing up. We are all on our way to somewhere. "On our way" means we're not there yet. Please forgive me for the parts in this book where that "not there yet" thing gets obvious. If you don't find Buddha in this book, it's because you've looked too far. Buddha is in you.

Dead Man Walking

Antisocial and better avoided.

Just one more last quick word of advice. This is not the most disturbing set of chapters ever written, but it certainly isn't the most enjoyable or intelligent one either. Ignorance, utter bullshit, gross stupidity, depression, ranting bitterness, and sophomoric immaturity make up most of the chapters of this section (although they are clever and entertaining in parts). This is a perfectly good book without them. Do yourself a favor and skip this section. If you do decide to read it, don't get used to the negative tone.

Surprisingly rapid improvements develop in the next section, "Meet the Family," as you meet the tribe of dedicated professional healers that surround the story. It has been a great privilege to be in the presence of these people. It will be an even greater one to introduce them to you—but the following bit of venom and mental illness happened first.

3

Suicide Note

I am gazing blankly through a second story window while writing this goodbye to no one. I watch the children laugh and play in the street below my window. They can't see me and they certainly can't see this writing. These kids have never spoken a word of English in their combined lives and wouldn't know what was on this paper if they were staring at it. But children still own sensibilities and sensitivities that adults have long ago thrown away. As I write this half assed explanation for my own murder, they suddenly stop playing to form a circle in the street beneath my window. They begin to cry and moan in harmony with each other, and in complete disharmony with the happiness they displayed just a minute ago.

Hungry shadows of failure swallow every thought. They stalk me and are gaining ground. Death's icy breath freezes my spine. The hundred and five degree tropical sun doesn't help. Too much pulse feeds crippling fear. Every breath brings more desperation and desolation. Death's breath is stronger than my own. Death's voice tells me to follow. I can't argue.

My mind replays old disasters. Everyone who has ever hurt me appears magnified into giants. Anger melts into depression as I have to admit that whatever they did to me, I let them do it. I've said "I'll be smarter next time" so often that I don't believe myself anymore.

Psychic beatings pay heavy karmic debts for trespasses I don't remember committing. Pain jumps from mind to land with both daggered feet on my chest. I wish it had gone on a diet first. A decayed giggle escapes as I realize there's nothing funny anymore. No thing.

Mind is prisoner within body. Hope surrenders. I'm no longer experiencing myself.

It is time to go.

4

Who Am I?

If I were dead it would all make more sense.

This hollow, fleshy beast I used to inhabit should logically be put down. He has done battle with life, not fared well, and is no longer functional. Trauma infects his mind and confusion fragments his heart. His character has decayed.

Some part of me knows that he and I are the same person, but that doesn't matter. I can't live with him anymore. We have already kicked each other out. We've just been too lazy and forlorn to finalize the separation.

How can I be so completely out of touch with everything beautiful and pleasant, yet so strongly and painfully in touch with repulsive emotions? Who stuck this shit in my head? It cannot be mine! Why am I so dangerously unbalanced, angrily depressed, and profoundly out of my fucking mind?

Less than a year ago, in America, I was a very popular and highly respected person. It seems ironic that a good part of that respect was earned by my work on behalf of troubled youth and psychiatric outpatients. There were also spiritual commitments, decades of effort on behalf of environmental groups, and a string of charity works long and strong enough to be featured in several newspapers.

Another part of that respect came from the admiration many folks had for my ability to smile most of the time, and to be kind and helpful as often as possible. I was so well trusted that over a dozen friends from New York City to Canada gave me their house keys, just in case I popped into their city when they weren't home. A key ring hung from my belt that would impress a K-Mart manager.

Yeah, I was a Class A do-gooder and as fine a friend as anyone could have. That's what folks told me. So how the hell did I get to be the asshole I am now? A winning lottery ticket couldn't raise my smile from the dead and it feels like a stranger lives in my body.

He is not a pleasant person.

I'll kill this stranger eventually, but there are more important things to deal with first.

The major problem is even more disturbing than having a jackass inhabit my body. It is bigger than not knowing exactly what happened or why. It is more painful than the sad fact that anything I can think of hurts.

The real problem is that I don't know what matters anymore.

5

What Does Matter

It doesn't matter if your skin is black, brown, red, yellow, white, or if you are from Europe, Asia, or North America. It doesn't matter if you are awkward, agile, thin, fat, blond, brunette, redhead, short, or tall. "Good looking" is an image that the fashion, fabric, and cosmetic companies invented so you'll buy things you don't need.

It doesn't matter if you're on the first page of a book or the last, reading or writing it—nor does it matter if you like pop, jazz, country, rock and roll, or classical music. The shill media industry only presents you with what their owners want you to see and hear. Most of us pay too dearly for limited, biased, dumbed-down content while enjoying the delusion that we choose from the best of all possibilities. Pre-Programmed Bullshit Package A and Pre-Programmed Bullshit Package B are your choices. They are both bullshit.

It doesn't matter if you are a lion, rabbit, elephant, giraffe, or gecko lizard. One of your cellmates or your Father Time is going to eat you. The best you can hope for is that the fuckers don't cage, sedate, and feature you on some TV nature channel first.

It doesn't matter if you and your kinky friends (as stated by the genius of George Carlin) "like to dress up in leather boy scout uniforms while you hit each other over the head with ball peen hammers and take turns blowing the cat. There's nothing wrong with that. It's a victimless hobby, and think how good it makes the cat feel."

Makes no difference whatsoever which brand of cigarettes you smoke, what side of a war you are on, whether your toxic waste is chemical or nuclear, or whether a scorpion or cobra bites you. You are still going to end up suffering too long, dead too quickly, or both.

It makes no difference at all which kind of unnatural drug you do. Whether you buy it from the street or it has been pharmaceutically prescribed, you're still going to enjoy a short high and then have to choose between hung over, dead, numb, addicted, or stupid.

It does not matter if you have a car that costs enough money to feed a small nation. Nor does it matter if you spend even more than that on a cocaine habit. It will matter even less when you land on your feet and ass at the same time as you come out of rehab a "cured," self-satisfied, self-righteous, self-indulgent pain in the ass of a person who never again does anything creative or constructive.

It doesn't matter one bit whether people believe you, like you, lie about you, love you, leave you, bait you, hate you, or rate you according to standards that are only badly pieced together fragments of their own personal hallucinations. If you believe that others' opinions of you matter, you lack strength, confidence, and structural integrity. You are attached to lies that aren't even your own.

So am I.

After the poison is added,
it doesn't matter if you eat health food or cake.

Do you know what does matter?

6

Temporarily

It seems we believe what we want to believe—making truth something we then need to retrieve. Wanting perfect love and life we seek perfect partners. We manufacture artificial gods and goddesses out of frail, flawed human beings. We allow imagination and desire to master over reality,

Temporarily.

Awakening from the liquid dream into the concrete nightmare we find there is no way to awaken from life. Addictive tendencies have attached us to manufactured circumstance. By grasping, we've lost our grip.

Living to discover life's solution becomes dying to release logic's prostitution as we face the facts just long enough to suffer dissolution of our beautiful but vanishing delusion.

We must now muster strength and make firm resolution to discover a solution to the intuitive pollution that fed our grand illusion and had us thinking we were sorrow-free,

Temporarily.

7

The Truth Can Wait

I would like to give every person who needs one a brand new childhood. I would say, "I'd like to ask God to give the folks that haven't enjoyed one a different, a happier childhood"—but God obviously isn't too bright. God thinks heaven and hell are in different places. Many humans aren't as bright as they could be either. A lot of that has to do with being scared of truth.

Humans too often allow superficial impressions to carry great weight.

"What it looks like" is deemed more important than "what it is." Reality is too often beaten into the back seat by opinion.

The truth can wait.

This applies all over the world of course,
whether you're the employee or the boss.

There are many who know that you will be more impressed by the wool they pull over your eyes than by what you would see without it.

Don't doubt it.
The truth can wait.

We believe what we want to believe, as if it were possible to self-deceive.

We live like prisoners in dreams of being free,
    glimpsing only shadows of a love we just can't see
        as we make believe that
            the truth can wait.

8

Answering the Right Questions,
Dodging the Right Bullet

Why does it seem that death might be more fun than life? Digging up a little background information might help me to figure this out. I'll bet my religion, government, schooling, the economic system I grew up under, and a lot of other people's bullshit has screwed me up worse than I could ever screw myself up. There have been a lot of assholes around here recently. It's probably their fault too!

But this mental decay is at least partly my fault and is now totally my problem. I'm incredibly lucid and savvy for a lunatic, but I also have to be one of the biggest fools in the galaxy. I came to Asia with the same foundationless hopes and lack of information that many people bring to their lives. Romancing a reality without knowing what that reality actually is has led us all to some painful surprises.

All the money consciousness and take-take attitude of the economically minded USA seems to be even more severe among the materialist wannabes here.

The racism seems more severe too.

Fact is, it was easier to be happy in America.

That's not the way this move was supposed to work. It's no wonder I'm depressed!

For decades I've rattled on about being a planetary citizen as opposed to being an American. This is not a slur against America. *Any* nationalism hides the deeper truth that we are all one people on one planet. Not treating the planet like a nation has too easily and often become a rationalization for not treating people like people.

This has caused a lot of suffering. Folks who used a blanket bad opinion of white foreigners to justify abusing them took advantage of me— and what I went through is a day at the beach compared to so many brutal examples that history offers.

The same type of trouble that found me here has found many others around the world. It can happen anywhere there are more have-nots than haves, which is almost everywhere. Wherever we find the belief that possession of more material stuff is the road to happiness, humanity's odds of overcoming the ugly extremes of self-interest decrease drastically.

Many people have bought into the very unfortunate human attitude of *entitlement*. Honorians are no exception. A person with this mindset thinks that they deserve better regardless of whether or not that betterment comes at the expense of another, or even at the expense of many others. This attitude accounts for how a lot of rich folks became rich. Many poor folks also picture this entitlement and material gain thing as the road to happiness. Some feel they just haven't been lucky enough to get into a position where they can profit by screwing others. I'm tired of watching it. I'm tired of people acting like nasty jackasses from one end of Earth to the other!

Many empires have embodied this attitude of entitlement over the years. America has been the standard-bearer for several decades. This goes a long way toward explaining the increasing disrespect and danger suffered by American tourists in recent years. Karma can be painful. People remember bombing raids for a much longer time than they remember relief efforts. A relief effort won't bring anyone's family back once they have been disintegrated. We thought ourselves entitled to trash a few places. Now they feel entitled to mess with us.

This happens at home as well as abroad. Our intra-national violations of the golden rule have resulted in us being nervous tourists in parts of our own country too. Many poor folks are so indiscriminately angry that it is not safe to walk through their neighborhoods.

Industrialists, banksters, corporations, and government shills have brutally cornholed America's growing poor and homeless populations as well as our shrinking middle class. Many disproportionately rich yet peculiarly unsatisfied people still feel entitled to make obscene profits regardless of the consequences to others. Foreign wars that kill our poorest teenagers, poison chemical dumping, substandard production methods using substandard materials, and mortgage fiascos that fall short of theft and fraud in only the most technical definitions of the law are just the tip of the iceberg.

Pardon the rant, but the point is that many developing nations throughout the world now cause and suffer the same problems as their Western economic and political role models. Nearly everything mentioned above is happening here and now in Southeast Asia.

No one seems able to learn a lesson. People are mad jackasses sometimes!

There are certainly other considerations besides my government's actions and policies that influence how our foreign neighbors view us, how they treat us when we visit their countries, and how I have been mistreated here.

Having enough money to afford the plane ticket to your third world destination qualifies you as rich on most of the planet, even if you consider yourself among the scrimp-and-save backpacker set. Couple this with the often held point of view that your wealth has resulted from your nation's exploitation of the rest of the world and it gets easier for someone to rationalize kicking your ass when they think you've been kicking theirs first.

The TV imaging of our Western lifestyle also helped to set me up as a mark. It sets up many of our traveling compatriots as marks throughout much of the world. Television often portrays us as wealthy, selfish, arrogant, violent, and apathetic. Evidence of that arrogance and apathy is too often presented on a silver platter to natives of the countries we tour. Many vacationers are demanding, drunk, or hung over more often than not. A handful become nasty and even the nicest Western tourists are spending enough money in a week to feed a third world family for a year.

I have to both sympathize with and be the victim of this international attitude problem! It is hard to take either side when both seem wrong. I've been picked on here for being an evil exploitative person, just because of my skin color and place of birth. But I've also been seated near some arrogant tourists whose behavior made me embarrassed to be American. I'm also aware of some history that is even more embarrassing than those tourists.

Honorian folks are very polite as a rule but as is true anywhere, there are some impolite bastards here who use inbred, bigoted notions to rationalize getting what they want by inappropriate or even criminally inconsiderate means. These people will never be able to see me as an individual because it fits their purpose or ignorance, or both, to view me as part of an evil machine.

The cultural introversion and occasional bigotry here may seem intense to a clever but mentally ill foreigner such as myself, who is counting on the kindness of strangers to stay alive—but as mentioned before, similar indecencies happen everywhere and are often much more severe. Most people in any country will go with the cultural flow of the status quo no matter how twisted popular attitudes may be. No matter how polluted the waters are, whether they include bigotry, slavery, theft, or even murder, people don't usually consider bucking the current to swim ashore.

People surely act like severe jackasses sometimes!

Come to think of it, I'm a people. I must be a jackass sometimes too.

I'm the fool wearing the *Mean People Suck* t-shirt who doesn't realize how mean-spirited that message is.

I better start dealing with how I am reacting to the situation here! It isn't possible to take out anyone else's mental garbage or change anyone else's shitty attitude—and there's no one else to blame if I keep wallowing in my own. Being trapped in this country doesn't have to include being trapped in my own toxic psychological sewerage.

It is time to figure out how to be nicer to myself and everyone else.

It is time to become less of a jackass.

The confusion of not wanting to stay here or go back to America is multiplied by not having the resources to do either. There is not enough money in my pocket to buy a beer at the local store, much less a plane ticket to America. I'm in the awkward position of having nowhere to go and no way to get there.

The life that I knew is over.

But *everything* is now a fresh possibility! The world is suddenly strange and different. There are no limits, no borders around what can happen next. Every experience is intensified. Life is vivid. Flowers scream out their color. Fragrances are powerfully defined. The air seems electrically charged and freshly invented, as if I'm the first one to breathe it.

The excitement of having no country and no money is electrifying.

The total freedom is magical.

It is also scarier than death.

I'm almost obliged to stay alive, just to see what happens next.

From the point of view of a man without a country or a dollar, it seems that the old saying is true. "Be careful what you ask for. You might get it."

I can't really blame my ragged situation on anyone, anywhere, or anything else but myself. I angrily blamed this country, the people in it, the climate, then my childhood, home country, and finally all of humanity.

None of it helped.

Blaming external sources for one's own bullshit is about as senseless as shooting oneself and blaming the bullet.

Not admitting that I had built my own life and its troubles robbed me of the ability to repair either—and it almost killed me.

Meet the Family

"Nirvana may be the final object of attainment,
but at the moment, it is difficult to reach.
Thus the practical and realistic aim is compassion,
a warm heart, serving other people, helping others,
respecting others, being less selfish."

The Dalai Lama

9

Chapter Dedication — Loving Kindness

As I was approaching death, a magic mental living breath
Flashed light into a tragic night, rekindling my extinguished sight
A shadowed message in my brain was wakened from within the pain
Softly spoken without word, that message was so clearly heard

Forgive, forget, just live and let...recall your ancient wisdom
It's sleeping now but we know how to unify your schism
Take heart and hope, untie your rope, and let your boat go sailing
Your ship is tight! Just do it right. There'll be no need for bailing

We cannot go there for you, as you must map your own path
(But we can help block broken roads and prevent aftermath!)
We're there; we care, and are aware of pain within your chest
Please take our kindness to yourself, as if your mother's breast

And when I rediscover health and take my life back off the shelf
They'll say I did it all myself with fortitude and mental wealth
They'll leave love there until it clicks, rebuild my house from broken sticks
Loving Kindness is the fix and Temple folk know all the tricks

10

A Few More Quotes by the Dalai Lama & Others

"Genuine satisfaction, genuine inner peace—you cannot buy through money and you cannot take by force. [It] only develops through training of mind, through *awareness*. The ultimate source of happiness, the ultimate source of a successful life, very much depends on our own mental state—irrespective of whether believer or non-believer."

"Buddhism/Dharma tradition is attracting many intellectuals and scientists—including some of the most well known in the world. They are not necessarily religious minded, but they are *really* showing genuine interest about the Buddha Dharma. So, I make a distinction. In the Buddhist texts, the explanation about mind, matter, and emotion have nothing to do with any positive or negative concept. They simply explain the reality. That part we should consider as *Buddhist Science*."

"Faith and prayer are very useful and helpful for individual peace of mind, but in the sense of the well being of the community and of the world, prayer has limitations. Buddha's blessing needs human action. Without human action, Buddha's blessing not much effective."

The Dalai Lama

"The old expression says 'History repeats itself.' It is true, but only if history is left to its own devices. Positive human intervention can, will, and must write a new history that replaces fear and injustice with a saner, more appropriate response to existence."

Tenzin Kharma Trinley

"This is a world of action, and not for moping and groaning in."

Charles Dickens

"I'm not going to tiptoe through life just to arrive at death safely."

Author unknown

11

Temple Dog Soldiers

I get along beautifully with the dogs at the Temple and the dogs at the Temple get along beautifully with life. There are about thirty of them. These dogs get fed and cared for better than many humans. Most also get along with each other better than humans do.

I associate with my canine buddies often. They're the only ones here who seem to understand English, but we have a lot more in common than just that. We all got the shit kicked out of us by life. Most of these dogs were abandoned in the mean streets and would likely be dead had benevolent passersby not brought them to the Temple. Yes, it is likely we would all have left the planet by now if not for the kindness and connections of someone who knew that "this dog belongs in the Temple."

I don't know if dogs are capable of actually *knowing* much but if they are, here are a few things these dogs know.

They are the luckiest sons of bitches in the Universe.

One minute of petting is better than years of getting kicked.

Mange, worms, tics, malnutrition, attack, and nonfatal injuries can all be classified as temporary setbacks.

They probably also think there is a God, or several of them.

Like the cat that just ate the canary, we stroll the grounds and wag our tales. We are barely smart enough to know that we have recently been given wings for no other reason than that we didn't have a leg to stand on.

We Temple dogs inadvertently get to be a little bit like soldier-type creatures guarding the outside perimeters of the residents' hearts.

It works like this.

No one expects us to do anything, much less do anything right.

We snap at flies and mosquitoes, pee on palm trees, don't speak the language, and are not physically able to do much work. Although we live in a Temple, nothing is expected of us in the technospiritual sense. We don't even know the words to the chants and prayers. Our happy hearts and healing bodies are pleasantly swollen with gratitude and good food, but these hearts and bodies are attached to very little in the way of a culturally functional brain.

When we fuck up, we don't even know that we have fucked up—and everyone around us knows that we don't know we've fucked up. This makes it easier for folks to practice their forgiveness and compassion. That makes them better-hearted people. We get petted and smiled at.

We often get petted and smiled at without fucking up! It can happen just because someone here wants to give kindness and affection to anything within range. That is what the people we live with do. It is more than just their job description. It is who they are.

I'm wagging, buddy. So are my dogs.

12

Darkness 1, 2, 3/First Days at Temple

ONE

Arjan has given me the rare privilege of enjoying some Monk benefits without having to take on monastic responsibilities. I have my own small concrete block bungalow on a hill overlooking the ocean. The water and bathrooms are downhill from the room.

The electricity went out in my bungalow last night. I lay down and felt the darkness. It was a warm, sensuous (that means something different in a Temple, folks) comforter that made nighttime a friend.

Half the Earth's time is spent soaking in darkness. Even if there's a full moon or big city lights, there is darkness. It is the darkness they are lighting up.

There are no big city lights here and there's no moon tonight. Without the vision that light affords, everything is left to the imagination. Beautiful dreams start in darkness.

It covers and nourishes each sensitivity with relief from daylight's harsher realities.

That's why creatures sleep so well in it.

TWO

Threatening.

I don't know what's out there.
There are monsters at the window.

Demons hide in the darkness.
They pop out to tear shreds from my small allowance of peace.
They leave pools of cold sweat and lonely panic behind.

Can't sleep.
Don't want to be awake.

Animal and insect noises sound like past hells revisiting to mock me.

Darkness laughs at my weakness but offers no options to it,
no escape from it.

I'm afraid my heart is going to explode.
I'm afraid to breathe.

I'm afraid.

THREE

A thought loud enough to be a voice tells me, "Get over it! There's nothing in darkness that isn't there in daylight. Cut both ends of this bullshit and go to sleep!" The thought is in English, but has an Honorian accent.

13

Gratitude

Most folks are grateful when something unusually pleasant comes along, great pain ends, or somebody does them a favor. People seem to save gratitude for special occasions.

The people who live at this Temple are grateful nearly all the time for whomever they are with and whatever they are doing at the moment. The Monks and Nuns remember what a lot of us have forgotten. Even when life seems to suck, there is probably something as well as someone in our life who deserves gratitude. That someone may not have physically done anything for us. They may only have encouraged us or wished us well. But a good thought is easier to catch than a bad cold, and a good thought can carry a person a very long way.

Gratitude has a powerful potential to multiply into a series of good events. I'm grateful for that, but then again I'm grateful for a lot of things. I'm too broke to get into the poorhouse and just a couple of weeks past suicidal, but a very highly respected spiritual leader has invited me into his community—no money down. Professional altruists care for me and a whole village feeds me. I'm doing very well for a dead guy. So when a wild errant thought still tells me that leaving life may be a better idea than staying with it, there is a pleasantly heavy load of gratitude balancing that errant thought.

I lean on it.

My debt of gratitude is owed to everyone who has put their generous effort into helping keep my boat afloat and teaching me how to adjust my sails to the wind. This debt will not be repaid by my untimely demise. That would make all their noble efforts wasted. And so, morbid thoughts must be replaced with better ones such as gratitude.

I guess whatever thoughts replace suicide are an improvement, but gratitude is special. Gratitude itself is so pure and good that it doesn't care if I use it as a crutch. Gratitude doesn't care what form it is used in. It's just grateful to be working.

I'm grateful that it's working too.

14

The Morning Walk

I have never looked forward to waking up at five a.m. I do now. The early Morning Walk sets a beautiful tone for the whole day. It is not the easiest job in the world, but it may be the most magical.

Technical definitions say that *monastics* stay to themselves and contemplate while *clergy* have more contact with parishioners. The ordained Temple dwellers here do both, so either title can apply. Many folks from the Western side of civilization would think of our Morning Walk simply as monastics begging for food. There's a lot more to it than that. There is also a strong element of clergy blessing their village.

Each Monk on the walk carries a covered bowl capable of holding about five pounds of cooked rice. The bowl is covered in the same orange or gold cloth that the Monk's robes are made of, as is the shoulder strap that secures it guitar style. Monks in training wear white suits and shoulder cloth bags. There are only two white-suited people in residence right now, a Monk in training named Mr. Mee and myself. I go on the walk by choice. Mr. Mee goes as part of his training.

At daybreak several Monks, Mr. Mee, and I walk together. Sometimes we walk silently, sometimes laughing and joking. Joking in sign and body language often makes the laughter sound louder and last longer than joking in spoken language would.

However light our mood appears, a deeper energy is building toward a much greater gravity. It feels something like those first few songs a band plays to build the atmosphere in a club before people actually start dancing. We walk down the Temple's dirt road into the network of narrow paths that have been carved by machete to connect the village. The paths contain sharp rocks, sticks, and the occasional deadly cobra or scorpion.

I'm the only one wearing shoes.

One of the narrow paths that connect the village

It is now about ten minutes after sunrise and the villagers are already awake. They are more than awake. They are prepared. Delicacies of vegetables with pork, beef, shrimp, fish, or squid are already cooked and packaged in small plastic bags fastened with rubber bands. The ever-present huge pot of rice is cooked to perfection. We white-suited folks are given the delicacies quietly and we put them into our shoulder bags.

On any given day we never get the same dish from any two villagers. I still don't know if they all get together the night before to talk about which dish each will prepare, or if it *just happens*. There are no bad cooks in Honoria. The quality, flavor, freshness, and variety of this daily feast are superior to what most professional buffet restaurants offer.

This is a fishing village by the ocean near a middle class tourist town. Most folks catch fish or can afford to buy meat. We are very fortunate. Many communities inland survive almost exclusively on rice. So do the Monks and Nuns in those communities.

At each house the family offers rice to the Monks. We students and observers in white suits get polite but minimal attention. The Monks lift the lids of their bowls and look intently at the scoops of white rice being offered into them, heads slightly bowed into the process. In wordless prayer they offer gratitude to the universe as well as to the sponsoring family.

You don't have to be a spiritualist or religious scholar to know that gratitude is happening. Gratitude is not a passing fancy to Buddhist clergy. It is recognized as part of the cycle of universal benevolence. These Monks have vowed to emulate this benevolence, not only in this singular lifetime but in their view, for eternity. They give their commitments to gratitude and compassion more gravity than they give to the concept of death. They spend as many hours meditating on these virtues as billiards professionals spend with their cue sticks. This type of gratitude is so potent that it can be easily felt, even in silence.

The family offering the food then gets into that deep native crouch that breaks white people's knees, with palms joined together and fingers pointed upward in the traditional prayer-style *Wai* position (with hands held at or above the forehead when in the presence of clergy or royalty). They then receive a spoken blessing from the Monks.

I have seen this happen many times, but the process never loses its power. There are times when the energy jumping between those bestowing and those receiving the blessing seems physically visible.

Gratitude (silent, then chanted) comes from the Monks who are receiving the food. It is directed first toward *everything* in spiritual and material existence, and then toward the individual sponsoring family. As the Monks' blessings are chanted, one can see the directional shift of human electricity taking place and feel the communion involved.

The Monks and the villagers actually alternate roles!

In Western culture, when someone gives something to us, we say "thank you." That's usually the end of the story. Maybe we get a "you're welcome," but the gratitude is pretty much moving in one direction. It goes from the receiver of the favor or sponsorship to the giver. That also happens in the Morning Walk, but then everything gets completely turned around in a graceful step of cultural religion that is a spiritual work of art.

The donating villagers are as grateful to the Monks for their blessings as the Monks have been to the villagers for receiving the food, kindness, and respect. The initial receivers of gratitude become the providers of it as the villagers bow to the Monks in gratitude for the blessings they have received. The circle of gratitude is complete. Our standard Western civil practice of "thank you" and "you're welcome" has been elevated into the realm of spiritual experience. The energy has multiplied.

The powerful merit and grace in our Morning Walk always leaves me with the feeling that I have just seen one plus one equal three.

15

More Scenes from the Morning Walk

16

As Does Bet

Monk Bet is one of my favorite people on the planet as well as being one of my favorites in the Temple. He is thirty three years old. *Bet* means "pole" in the Honorian language. Compared to most Honorians, Bet resembles a skyscraper more than a pole. He is six feet and five inches tall, kind, graceful, playful, and always happy and smiling. The puppies come running when they see him. So do most people.

This afternoon Monk Bet found out that his older brother (also a Monk, but at a different Temple) died in a train wreck yesterday. He tried to explain this to me, but I couldn't understand what he was saying. He was smiling. I still know very little of the Honorian language and Bet knows about five words of English, but language wasn't the only communication problem. His pleasant attitude was completely out of sync with the tragedy he was talking about. I wouldn't have understood him had he been speaking perfect English!

Bet gave up on the communication. He wrapped it up with an amused giggle and one of the few phrases that he sort of knows in English. "Chust choking." ("Just joking.")

Mr. Mee and a Nun's assistant named Kumnung, with much effort and sign language, explained everything to me this evening.

By then, Bet had already left for the bigger Temple down the road where his brother's funeral will be held in a day or two. I'd like to go comfort him, but he already seems to be taking the news a lot better than I am. It is certainly not because he didn't care about his brother or because he thinks life is cheap. Bet spends his entire existence being grateful for his birth and trying to lighten the suffering of his fellow creatures.

The stability of his unshakable faith has its advantages. Being a living definition of strength also has advantages, as does having a deep understanding that *all* things must pass.

As does Bet.

I'm sure his brother did too.

Meals will be served at the usual time tomorrow but everyone will eat whatever is already in the kitchen, or what grasses and herbs we can pick from the hillsides.

We won't make our Morning Walk without Bet.

Monk Bet carrying water

17

Tah Mak Wat Lo (Our Senior Monk)
At Bet's Brother's Funeral

This mystic's eyes project goodness and pure compassion to every thing. They erase boundaries between thought and function that most of us would consider impenetrable.

A look into these eyes dissolves disaster. A look away is necessary— as necessary as it would be to look away from the power of stadium lights.

He remains an unassuming, cooperative part of a stage filled by nine Monks. Nine bodies meld into a singular brainheart while the individuality of each remains stable and apparent as well.

Our senior Monk transcends ordinary reality and sits, somehow, both facing and between the two surviving brothers of the deceased. The chanting begins. As the intensity grows, he erases anything amiss in the UniVerse by simultaneously striking The Lost Chord as an individual and in concert with his fellow Monks. He extends his heart to his junior partner with an intensity that we normal, untrained humans simply don't have access to. It is just as well that we don't. Without proper training, a heart stretched with that degree of conviction might be irretrievable. But Monk Tah Mak Wat Lo has been in training for many years. Emotional Instability lost our Senior Monk's address a long time ago.

I've had a toothache all day. I see Tah Mak Wat Lo's tongue move across a tooth that is in the same spot in his mouth as the one in my mouth that is causing me pain.

The pain disappears from my tooth.

Magic lives in our Senior Monk.

Monk Tah Mak Wat Lo

18

Monk Tommy

Tommy is a very rare person. He is a Caucasian Monk in Asia, an expatriate Swiss national. Tom is, in a word, brilliant. He speaks German, Honorian, English, French, and Italian fluently. A year ago he lived in the Temple where I now live. He has just returned for a short visit.

Tommy had to leave our Temple long before his technical Buddhist education was completed. So many people were coming to him for counsel that Arjan had to move him to a more isolated Temple in order to continue his studies without interference. Tom can help a person make sense out of the seemingly senseless. He can freshen up old, clichéd logics so they sound like revelations again. Whenever Tommy is present, I consider it a gift.

We hung out for about an hour today as he humbly performed his conversational magic. I was rattling on about racism, good guys versus bad guys, and the whole nine negative yards. He spoke about the weeds being "as lovely as the flowers, to Nature itself—it's just because of our attachments to what we consider beauty that we see one as more beautiful than the other," and "transcending the dualism," and "relative realities," and "nonattachment to self," etc. That's my minimalist phrasing, of course, not his. There's no possibility of me relaying the wisdom of Tommy's stories with the depth and clarity he accomplishes. Everything he says leads back to the point that life can be very good if we take control of our own loose ends and tie them together well.

Everything Monk Tommy says is probably true, but I still can't absorb or live by a lot of it. This may be because my head is still too far up my ass to altogether focus on the bright side of things. I still haven't been able to eliminate righteous indignation or even anger from my little brain.

I'm not alone. All the combined beauty of cosmic reality wouldn't make a rat's ass worth of difference to that child in Tibet who had a rifle shoved into his hands by Chinese soldiers and was ordered to shoot his parents. It might not help that seven year old black kid who had his penis cut off and stuffed in his mouth by the KKK, either. It doesn't even help ease my childhood memory of hearing about the heinous event. So many people are separated from their best life and happiest thoughts by circumstances that seem to be completely beyond their personal control. That can piss anyone off.

Tom and I both want to believe what he believes, and we both know the truth and horror of what I've seen and heard.

We both know that almost nothing is pure black or white. Earth happenings are nearly always a shade of grey. "One man's ceiling is another man's floor," as Paul Simon said. There is no pure right or wrong except in the eye of the beholder.

We also both know that even the most righteous indignation is still indignation. Indignation is always a burden to the person who carries it, and it never accomplishes as much as appropriate action would.

In the final analysis, Tommy's positive and accepting attitude is certainly the more attractive one to live by. But most of us don't get to the final analysis. We usually spend a lot more time in the kickass physical world than we spend in the more blissfully transcendent realms. I guess that's our own fault. The world may, as Shakespeare said, be a stage, but no one else dictates our location or writes our script for us—and our editing power is limitless. We can have our minds in those more transcendent frames if we put them there.

I think I'm going to spend more time hanging out with Tommy.

(Ssshh! Don't tell! I think Monk Tommy is an ET!!!)

Monk Tommy

Monk Tommy's monthly shaving ritual

Monk Tommy, always positive and accepting

19

Why the Monks and Nuns Are Who They Are 1

THE BIG BRAIN THING

"In the cultivation of the mind, our emphasis should not be on concentration, but on attention. Concentration is a process of forcing the mind to narrow down to a point, whereas attention is without frontiers."

J. Krishnamurti

The locals visit our Temple often. Some come on to the grounds screaming, crying, angry, depressed, or agitated. After a half hour of talking with our Wisdom Professionals, the formerly forlorn usually leave smiling.

Why do so many people come here to see the robe wearers, and why do all these visitors leave feeling so much better than they did upon arrival?

Why are the residents of this Temple so much fun to be around?

What makes the Monks and Nuns who they are?

There must be some reasons I'll never know, but a few are obvious. The first is The Big Brain thing, and the team spirit it entails. The second is reincarnation—but probably not the kind of reincarnation you are used to hearing about. These two meet at so many crossroads that it is often hard to separate them, but let's try to take them one at a time, starting with The Big Brain thing.

Everybody's got a brain and a mind. Many people consider these to be different words for the same thing. Technically, the brain is just a biological organ while the mind is something deeper and more inclusive, but if it makes you comfortable we can use these words interchangeably. It won't hurt anything. The words *soul* or *spirit* might also be accurate, and *consciousness* is actually what we're talking about—but some folks think of these terms as abstractions. Let's use the more familiar words *mind* and *brain* for now. Many folks find those references more comfortable.

It is widely known that any human uses only a small percentage of his or her mind/brain at any given time. Exactly how much gets used and what those percentages pay attention to have always been very important matters.

The Monks and Nuns believe that each individual carries a responsibility to focus the greatest possible percentage of their mental facility on the best attitudes and functions they can produce. Fulfilling this responsibility is not optional. It is mandatory for them, as it probably should be for all of us. They recognize this responsibility as a necessity because it affects all individual, familial, societal, and planetary relationships as well as our survival. Directing the use of our minds toward constructive positive ends is not an esoteric or saintly activity. It's a practical and logical one. Material and emotional satisfaction are most comfortably born of mental satisfaction. Happy and compassionate people don't normally steal from or kill each other.

Whether conscious of it or not, we always think of an action before we do it. It seems there are major advantages to thinking consciously. The residents here know that any action should be avoided if it doesn't help. Blind emotions lead many folks to destructive actions. There are no blind emotions here. By quieting mental turbulence, these folks clearly see what they are thinking, and then steer it. Everything they do is done on purpose. Nothing ever *gets away* from them.

The sub or unconscious type of thought and action is usually fueled by instinctive reactions or habitually programmed mental reflex reactions.

The most basic are survival instincts and callous self-interest—animal reflexes. All of us live at least partially under direction of such instincts. Our DNA has carried these base instincts since the caveman days.

There are other characteristics and instincts that we have inherited through training and information we have been given. These are the conditioned reflexes—behavioral patterns we have observed and absorbed since birth.

These biological and historical patterns coexist as what can be called *the little brain*. A lot of human actions could more accurately be called knee jerk reactions. Many people spend most of their lives controlled by mental patterns that they are not even aware of.

But we have all floated into *The Big Brain Thing* on occasion.

The Monks and Nuns live there. Their conscious focus is on the mind and life that we all share in our involuntary coexistence with all other creatures—animal, human, and divine. They are of the opinion that the similarities and relationships between us all are more deserving of attention than the differences. They believe that the mutually beneficial goals that this Big Brained point of view dictates outweigh personal goals in importance.

This concept of humanity sharing a mutual and universal mind resembles Carl Jung's Collective Unconscious theory—except with the Temple folks it is conscious, it has been around several thousand years longer, and it is considered fact, not theory.

This makes a big difference.

The drop/ocean metaphor is often used to explain this.

Most of us think of ourselves as an individual drop of humanity. The people here in the Temple think of themselves as an integral part of a vast ocean. Both views have truth in them. This "ocean" attitude may seem a little esoteric or even weird to many of us, but it has advantages. Individual problems and personal pains recede when you are paying attention to the bigger picture. The freedom and security that the power of an ocean offers is much greater than that of a single drop of water, or a singular human.

Like most of us, the Temple residents have good intentions. They are more committed to their good intentions than most of us are to ours. They make that commitment functional by donating their motivation for achievement toward improving life for all of their fellow creatures. They constantly work on improving their little drop (self), but that process is always based on how their drop can become a better drop in order to become part of a better ocean (how their lives can improve *all* lives). They do the dancing with their own legs, but a force much bigger than any individual is always playing the tune. All ways.

To put it another way, these Wisdom Professionals have trained their little brains very thoroughly in the concern for *all* little brains. This puts them on the same wavelength with, and keeps them tuned to the same station as, that bigger force that both contains and is concerned with the well being of all the little brains—The Big Brain. They have, through dedication and severe effort, actually become a conscious cell in and therefore a co-creating partner with The Big Brain.

In this sense it can be said that they have *become* the Big Brain. Call it God, Dharma, The Force, the Collective Unconscious, the Unified Field. Whatever you would call an all inclusive divine resource, they are now part of it. Their loyalties and actions are as concerned with the ocean at large as they are with their own individual drop. This affiliation with and incorporation into the Big Brain governs the lives of the Nuns and Monks, and the choices they make. It directs them as surely as any commander directs his troops.

For a few minutes after figuring this out, I wondered why these folks weren't a bit more uppity. Merging with God seems like it would give one bragging rights. Why is there no pretense? Why no arrogance? There is no "I'm so great because I do this." Just a whole lot of "I'm a person just like you."

With just a little more thought it became obvious to me why modesty has to be a part of their package. When one lives by the idea that we are all one big interdependent unit even more than we are our individual bit of self, it is hard to feel superior or snooty. If you are thinking in terms of *everybody* instead of *somebody*, then you have an automatic empathy with all and cannot be more (or less) important than anyone else. If you hit anybody, you are hitting your own body. If you mistreat or take undue advantage of anyone, you are also mistreating and unduly taking advantage of yourself. The Nuns and Monks walk humbly in this knowledge and they carry a great consideration for all forms of life.

As a trained and dedicated part of a much bigger whole, they can often rise above what would be thought of as the usual human limitations. We all reach this state and the power it holds on rare occasions and in varying degrees. We all know stories about folks tapping into some greater power. We've heard the tales of superhuman strength, of lifting a car to save someone trapped underneath.

We all work through days when we feel dog-sick and tired and it should not be possible to even get to work, much less stay through the day. But we reach deeper for strength because the kids we love need to be fed, or someone else we care about depends on us to bring that paycheck home.

Where does this magic come from? It comes from an attitude brave, concerned, and smart enough to travel past the point of view that makes us each individual drops instead of an ocean. It comes from considering your loved one to be as important as yourself, and from believing in that strongly enough to erase the boundaries between. It comes from floating the little brain into The Big Brain.

The Monks and Nuns live in this bigger context full time. Anyone is everyone to them. Their concern is universal.

Another reason why the Monks and Nuns are who they are is that they consistently reflect upon the benefits of compassion and make effort to keep compassionate thoughts in mind. The major part of this reflection is the intent to help any living thing that needs help. By means of this constant intending and reflecting (and then acting in accord with those intentions and reflections), a habitual pattern of going past the self-interest, self-referral way of thinking is built intentionally. Being aware of their own thoughts and consciously piloting their own actions allows these people to direct their efforts toward entraining benevolent behavior as habit.

Not consciously directing one's own thoughts and actions, not being aware of the quality of those thoughts and actions, steals from the person performing those actions the ability to consciously entrain that behavior as habit—to tell the little brain that this is a Big Brain thing, we like doing these aware-and-benevolent sorts of things, and we should stay awake to opportunities to do them more often.

Things that are done on purpose carry greater weight.

Another key point for entering The Big Brain seems to be fearlessness—a confidence in one's ability to grow more inclusive, to include others into your world view, and to realize the equality of everyone in that we are each as deserving of happiness as the other. It can be scary to step past your borders in the face of maintaining the necessary ego strength for intelligent survival. These Wisdom Professionals accomplish fearlessness in the same way they accomplish most things—through extensive training in compassion. They foster a concern for others that both overrides and accomplishes their own personal needs.

It's easy for people to forget personal fears when they are helping others, or even thinking about helping others. While busily extending themselves for the benefit of everyone, Nuns and Monks rarely suffer personal drama, trauma, or distress from any discomfort they may experience. Some types of pain happen to everyone, but the suffering that is a byproduct of that pain can be minimized. Within the bigger and more altruistic picture, a smaller and more personal problem can't gain the gravity of a major concern. Imaginary, intangible, and exaggerated fears cannot take hold.

Many universal abilities ride along with this universal concern. It is an instant antidote to reckless selfishness and the disasters that selfishness can foster.

Benefits including contented kindness and increased mental power come from being in this oceanic state of mind. These benefits grow in proportion to how much concern we have for each creature in the metaphorical ocean and how wisely we use that concern to benefit creatures. "You've got to be a friend to have a friend." Amoebas, whales, heroes, villains, ants, eagles, enemies, allies, and anything else that is alive are each considered important parts of the much bigger picture.

The Temple residents have faith in the abilities of humanity. They believe we can each get bigger than our present selves, redefine "normal," and achieve greater happiness consistently. We have the internal technology. There is no doubt in the mind of anyone who lives here that you and I can do this. They believe that every one on Earth has the potential to improve their own lives in a way that will improve all the lives around them. They believe any person can ignore this positive potential and become evil, or compliant with evil. They also believe that any one of us can take this positive potential to its ultimate destination and become a buddha him or her self. It is just a matter of consistently choosing to exercise the best options and opportunities available.

Another quality that makes these Temple residents who they are is gratitude. They are aware of and grateful for how much other people are constantly doing that benefits them, and they know that each of us is dependent upon all of us for what we eat, drink, wear, and how peacefully or not we get to live. We are all part of this interdependent bigger picture whether we are aware of it or not. They are.

Thoughts like these are the exercise that Monks and Nuns use to accept all living things into their field of concern. This concern was the seed motivation for many of them to enter the clergy. It is now the final destination for all of them. They believe that we all move a step closer toward Big Brain, big happiness, and big constructive power every time we do, pray for, focus on, or even simply remember things that include good intent and no harm.

By the time a Monk, Nun, or anyone else gains enough familiarity with these ideas to metabolize them, so-called magic and synchronicity can become pronounced and obvious.

That may sound a little far fetched to many Western minds. It did to mine, at first. But the longer I stay here at this Temple, the more obvious it becomes that the Monks and Nuns are on to something of universal importance and incredible potential.

What they do and who they are is similar to a very good doctor. They develop the skill, experience, and intuition to diagnose and treat more effectively by studying every aspect of treatment and practicing a continuous concern for each individual patient. The spiritual doctors here don't push drugs or surgery. They cause no harm to anyone and show no preferential treatment for the wealthy. This adds legitimacy and strength to their healing abilities. *Genuine* universal inclusion has power.

We don't have to be a Monk, Nun, or Dr. Schweitzer to take part in this process. This is not a Santa-Claus-eligible fantasy story where only "special people" succeed. It is a proven scientific process of utilizing a potential we all own. There are specific methods that will work for anyone who practices them long and diligently enough. Anyone making effort can expand happiness in their own lives and any other lives they touch.

When a person desires to help everything and dedicates his or her life to that purpose, it is in every thing's best interest to help that benevolent person succeed. The world will then become a cooperative partner. Life is on that person's side. Life itself and these Wisdom Professionals have a common and mutually beneficial purpose. They assist each other to accomplish mutually beneficial goals.

This cooperation is the root system of magic.

The folks here are driven to deeds of goodness as a natural result of *being* goodness. That is the kind of people they decided to be, and what they have become through their training. That is why they are who they are.

Welcome to the Big Brain Team. Altruism is not optional. The system doesn't work without it. (Don't get nervous about your little personal things as you give your efforts to the whole. The ocean will take care of the drops that take care of the ocean. It's a physics thang.)

"To embody the transcendent is what we are here for."

Sogyal Rinpoche

"Matter is less material and the mind less spiritual than is genuinely supposed. The spiritual separation of physics and psychology, mind and matter, is metaphysically indefensible."

Bertrand Russell

20

Mr. Mee and Ms. Kumnung

Mr. Mee and Ms. Kumnung are my best friends in the Temple. He is a Monk student. She is a Nun's assistant and lay disciple. That means she does all the things a Nun student would do but is not planning to actually become one. Neither Mee nor Kumnung drink alcohol, have sex, eat after noon, or partake in many of the things that most of us would consider daily habits, pleasures, or even necessities. They are both happy.

They are like parents, a brother and sister, and friends to me. They help me with my language handicap and never call me "farang." We eat together and breathe together. When one of us leaves the Temple grounds, we miss each other. I go out from the Temple grounds often. They rarely leave at all. In spite of my financial destitution, I always share tobacco with Mr. Mee and make special efforts to get sweets for Ms. Kumnung. She smiles when I come back from town, whether I'm carrying sweets for her or not. I would miss a hundred meals just to see that smile once.

Mr. Mee is the James Brown of our Temple home. Just like the late, great "hardest working man in show business," he is constantly making an effort. With tools that would be considered more of a liability than an asset in the Western world, he gets everything done. Raking, hoeing, planting, painting, studying, and cleaning—he does it all and more. There is no lawn mower here. He mows the large lawn with a scythe and scissors.

Neither of these people ever complains about anything although more often than not there are no sweets, and some days we have no money for rolling papers. Mr. Mee and I often make our cigarettes from shreds of calendar paper and donated tobacco.

Mee and Kumnung always try to understand me. This takes all their patience, but they somehow never run out of it. There is very little I wouldn't do for them and it seems they each feel the same way toward me.

Mr. Mee has enough scars on his arm from heroin addiction to have scared the shit out of Kurt Cobain and Lenny Bruce.

Ms. Kumnung has both heart and lung malfunctions. She takes more prescription medication than any nursing home resident I've ever met.

Mee and Kumnung are married. They shared the same bed for eight years before coming to the Temple to sleep apart.

I guess they think things are better this way.

My Sister Kumnung

21

The Living Yahk

You probably don't know what a Yahk is. I'm not sure I do either, but here's my understanding of it. The Yahk is one of Honorian Buddhism's symbolic deities. Yahk is the great protector. He is most often depicted in statues as standing with knees bent and both hands clasping a sword, its tip planted in the ground between his feet. Benevolence for the objects of its protection beam from the Yahk's image, as does a severe warning for potential adversaries.

The Yahk has a strength of body, mind, and spirit that are obvious immediately and become more so over time. The courage of a thousand lions is at home in the Yahk. It offers protection not only from accidents and enemies but also from deeply damaging memories, psychological pain, spiritual misdirection, self-sabotaging behavior, and malnutrition of the heart. It has, for each of its charges, the love and vigilance that Joan of Arc had for her God and her people combined. The Yahk is invincible, and when you are in contact with the spirit of the Yahk you feel invincible too.

Yahk Amulet

Monk Chaiyote gave me a Yahk amulet.
He has the moral authority to give these to people.
Chaiyote is a Yahk himself.
He gave me permission to take this photo of him.
I treasure it even more than I treasure the amulet.

Monk Chaiyote

22

Miss Tiem A – True Nun

It took months before I realized who this walking enigma was!

Her silken gentility houses a pristine clarity of mind that broadcasts wordless comfort. Her whispered depth is filled with strength and kindness. She emanates a silent "I love you" in all directions, at all times, toward everything.

Every thing.

I feel it from a hundred yards behind me and don't have to turn around to know—

She's there.

Miss Tiem

23

Monk Sohn

Some folks are *naturals*. This doesn't mean that they don't have to work. It just means that they seem to have been born to do whatever it is they are doing. Willie Mays or Roberto Clemente in baseball, Bill Hicks and George Carlin in comedy, Tina Turner and Beyonce in music and dance all started with strong natural gifts. Of course, they added a lot of applied effort. Even the most naturally talented folks have to bust ass to be great.

We have a twenty one year old chanting phenomenon at the Temple who is one of these people. Monk Sohn is one of Nun Tiem's five sons. (She was not always a Nun.)

Sohn's physical appearance would have you guessing that he is a child, but his powerful presence makes a good argument for reincarnation. He may be nine million years old, in spiritual terms.

As is true of most Honorian Monks, Sohn is as Honorian as he is Monk. That means that he is happy and playful about his religion as well as everything else. He lives by the principles of Emma Goldman's famous statements, although he has certainly never heard of her. "How serious you are has nothing to do with how serious you are." "If I can't dance, I don't want to be part of your revolution."

Sohn must have matched his natural inclinations toward fun and chanting with a lot of focus and sustained hard work. This focus and work has ripened Sohn's natural talent into a master's level of accomplished potential. It is very unusual for a person as young as Sohn to have earned the admiration of so many senior Monks.

Even when Sohn is just silently walking, electricity can be felt in the atmosphere around him. When he's chanting, it is intoxicating to all who hear him.

Monk Sohn's talents are most obvious during the nightly chant. There is a short preliminary chant/blessing performed between individual pairs of Monks, when the group first sits on the raised platform in front of the Temple's shrine figures. This process is about each Monk empowering himself as well as the other Monk in his pair. A junior and senior Monk face each other and chant quietly, building an energy designed to increase spiritual connection and intensity. That energy is then used to invoke a good will towards and happiness for all living things.

Sohn is always paired with and facing the Arjan. No one in this Temple would be surprised if it was somehow proven that the roles of these two as junior and senior were reversed in a previous lifetime.

During this short preliminary, the junior Monk, with head bowed, chants to the senior. The senior responds briefly. It goes back and forth like this for about ten minutes. Sohn's chant is always the most softly sung but the most loudly felt. It is also sung quickly, as if he has known his lines by heart for a very long time. It's not an apathetic speed chant for the purpose of finishing fast. It is the most beautiful and melodic of any song in the Temple. It would compare favorably to one of the subtler guitar solos of a master such as Chet Atkins, Jimi Hendrix, or Pat Metheny.

When this introductory portion is complete, all Monks face forward again and the actual evening service begins. At this point Sohn's voice becomes the most evident in volume and lyrical command as well as sheer beauty and inspiration. He's feeling it. He's *really* feeling it! The most authoritative voice in the choir comes from its youngest member.

Monk Sohn

Our junior brother is eons older than he appears—and his voice was born from the heart of Music itself.

Monk Sohn

24

Master Teacher

Arjan Dang is our Head Monk. He has an amazing intuitive sense that allows him to completely adjust his conversation to each individual person or situation. It's a lot easier to help someone if both of you are on the same wavelength. Arjan seems to know how to get on to anyone's wavelength. His unstained concern allows him to override what we would think of as a normal separation of mentalities. I have seen him exercise this sensitivity many times. He has given me things *as I have thought about* asking for them.

Imagine how special you might have to be to teach broken folks how to become whole and enslaved people how to become free, or to help piece together a family that's torn, or rescue a heart from damaging scorn.

This master teacher is no mere preacher. He speaks wordless volumes of crystalline logic with no pretense. No quoted scripture or affected flash of the eye is necessary to impress, as he adjusts his reality to feel and then heal your distress. Multiple styles and rhythms in a single song pronounce definitions of gentle-yet-strong while he's lending his right to the part you got wrong.

He charges no fee. He requests nothing.

Master Teacher can give you a ride to your destination while you drive your own car, whether it's pointed toward a church or a bar. He teaches how to read life's maps, and that not speeding is the best way to avoid speed traps. He explains why not speeding can often get us to where we are going faster than speeding will. Master Teacher is not reading from any spiritual text or magically exorcizing the hexed. He detects just what vexes you and reveals why, while he teaches your thoughts how to self-clarify.

As the smoke clears from what you were thinking, you now can clean up what was stinking and rejuvenate what was shrinking. Master Teacher helps you to resolve strife and enjoy life to its fullest potential. This allows joy to stay self-repairing. It inspires greater decency and increased sharing.

The effects of a human life can be more frightening than lightning and thunder under ordinary circumstance. This Master teaches extraordinary resilience as an ordinary circumstance and in this way beats fear at its own game.

Esoteric yet down to earth, product of stable and daily rebirth, he facilitates growth without the fertilizer. Master Teacher is a quantum realizer.

Many come to Arjan seeking help in finding *the light*. The light itself looks forward to seeing him. He and the light share the same root system. Master Teacher is the fruit of humanity's finest tree.

Arjan Dang, Head Monk and Master Teacher

25

Why the Monks and Nuns Are Who They Are 2

REINCARNATION

Two Schools of Thought

"Isn't it enough to see
that a garden is beautiful
without having to believe
there are fairies
at the bottom of it too?"

Douglas Adams

When Eleanor Roosevelt was asked for her thoughts about reincarnation, she answered, "I don't see why it would be any more surprising to find myself in another life than it is to find myself in this one."

Jacques Cousteau's answer to the same question was, "Let's not think about that now. Nobody knows! Let's concentrate on the things we can feel and see and take care of right here, right now. The other will take care of itself later."

The concept of reincarnation as the rebirth of a migrating soul, spirit, or consciousness into a new body after the death of its previous body makes sense to some folks. Many reserve judgment. To others it is a fairy tale.

What is usually presented to us as the Buddhist concept of reincarnation may not be the whole (or even the real) picture. The Buddha's lesser known concept of reincarnation needs to become better known. It is practical, important, offers great opportunities, and cannot possibly be seen as a fairy tale.

What is this feet-on-the-ground concept of reincarnation? It starts with the idea of karma. Karma is not some fantastic mystical force that is controlled by magical beings. It is an earth-real part of natural law that expects to be influenced directly by the creatures it governs. "Karma," literally translated, simply means *action,* but within our context it also implies a *re-action* or the results of action.

The Buddha agreed with the existing ideas that the society of his time associated with the term *karma*—that everything most humans experience is a result of causes and conditions that lead to actions fostering effects that produce more causes and conditions, what goes around comes around, you get what you have paid for in some fashion, and so on. But he added a very important aspect to those concepts.

The major aspect he added is *the end of karma.*

A desire leads us to a thought that leads us to an action. If we choose to not take that action, that action is finished before it starts—it never exists. By doing this we prevent the action itself and the karma that would have followed. We disassemble the chain that keeps the karmic effect going, the usual chain reaction that *would have* seen that original action be the cause for another effect and lead to another desire or thought, and then more action on behalf of that desire-sponsored thought, and on, and on.

This universal law has been described in a thousand ways in a million places and can be as simple as "I think I like it, I'll go get it, I have used it up, I miss it, I still like it and want more of it, I'll go get..." in the attachment/like/desire connotation. On the other side of that same coin is the aversion/hate/fear scenario. "I don't like that, I'll go where it isn't, oops it showed up here too and it is always on my mind, I'll get away to where it isn't again, well there it is again (or there's something similar to it in my brain), so I have to get away from it again or spend a lot of time and trouble not liking or even hating it while it's stuck in my mind and life..."

This process can play out in many ways. An uncontrolled attachment to something can cause a person to take drastic, even immoral or dangerous action to obtain the object of desire. People often suffer greatly when an object of their affection is unobtainable or a desire is unattainable.

> *"Whenever there is attachment,*
> *association with it brings endless misery."*

Gampopa

A negative emotional response toward something can cause a person to take drastic action to avoid that something, and cause suffering when stuck in its presence. Both the repercussions and the side effects of these drastic actions and sufferings can warp our view of things and lead to many additional problems.

> *"For example, when you are describing a certain person to others, if he is your friend, you will only mention his good qualities; but if you dislike him, you will only point out his faults and not mention his good qualities. Tainted by attachment and aversion we cannot see how things really are."*

H.E. Garchen Rinpoche

A good method of breaking these chains of conditioned reaction is described within the practical and functional Southeast Asian Buddhist definition of daily-use reincarnation.

Pardon some repetition here, but this can be a difficult concept to understand. It was for me! Maybe looking at it from another angle will help.

I have saved money for a year to buy a car. A dealer sells me a lemon. I get pissed off and think to drive the car through his showroom window and crush the jackass beneath my defective wheels. I get past the blind emotion and become aware of this thought before acting on it—and then dismiss it without allowing it to become an action. I am aware enough to catch my mind going postal and change it before it does. I do not go crazy, knowing that it would make things worse in the long run. This avoids the possibilities of getting hurt, hurting others, ending up in jail, and what would no doubt be a long and complicated chain of ugly trouble. I can now take a different and more practical action that might have a much better outcome than my craziness would have produced.

It's that simple. The trick seems to be in the consistency. It is an easy decision for most folks to not drive a car through a window and crush a jackass. But there's a lot that just gets away from our attention, and that's the stuff that becomes the knee jerk reactions and attitudes. Everything from destructive consumer habits to artificial fears, racism, and more can fall into this category. Many of us feel that our lives are out of our own control. It is unlikely that the external forces we fear are actually controlling us. It is more likely that we are being steered by an undesirably conditioned and often self-defeating autopilot within.

The Monks and Nuns think it better to stay aware of their thoughts, emotions, and motivations as these feelings arrive in the present tense. This can be a lot more constructive than reacting from a mental attachment to the conditioning of an often suspect personal history. This allows them to clearly see any given situation for what it is, instead of how they feel about it. It allows more options of behavior and attitude that are born of choice, and it allows them to move their lives in the direction they want their lives to go.

Every action has consequences that are both immediate and continuing, so it is important to steer anything and everything from negative to positive, and to divert all of our traumatic reactions toward stability.

The idea of breaking the chain at any particular thought before it becomes an action isn't to bring the world to a standstill. The idea is to bring that errant thought to a standstill so we can start fresh with a new and more constructive thought that will lead to a better action. This prevents that first undesirable thought from ever turning into an undesirable action that will come back to bite us in the ass.

In essence, we reincarnate that thought.

Rebirth, reincarnation, the reformation of your life, or whatever you want to call it, happens at the moment of action every time we do something. No matter how big or small a thing we do, karma is created by it and the mind and life of the person taking that action changes as a result, right then and there. We start again from that moment as that new person, with that new addition to our character.

The addition may be barely noticeable, or it may be massive enough to alter history.

There are similarities here to the ceremony of baptism or the Born Again Christian approach. The similarity ends as participants in this Southeast Asian Buddhist approach continue practicing rebirth with every thought they have and every action they perform. This is not a one shot ritual and then back to business as usual.

The Monks and Nuns here constantly stay on this mental rebirthing in the hope of attaining a complete, indelible, and irreversible realization. The realization they aim for says that in each new moment, thought, and action is housed the opportunity for a completely new start. This new start opens to a realm of unlimited potential choices and attitudes.

Consistent freedom from conditioned habitual response fosters the ability to access happiness, kindness, and many other benefits at will. When a mind fires up freshly to every thought and is empty of congestive history, that mind is free to choose its own motives.

Picture the amount of constant work it takes to remain in the entrapment and repetitive grind of this attachment/aversion lifestyle where most of us unconsciously spend much of our lives. It leaves us hanging like addicted puppets on borrowed strings, constantly battling to fix things while we break them. This process can self-perpetuate indefinitely if no intervention is taken. It leads to unavoidable suffering, as we will always be either trying to get more of or get away from something external to ourselves. We are therefore never completely satisfied, altogether happy, or totally at home in our own skins.

It also takes work to be consistently aware of one's own thoughts, but at least there are good results from it! When we are more aware of the forces that drive us, we gain greater control of ourselves. As we start doing things on purpose, the conditioned ways of being and self-centered loves and hates do not direct us anymore. We start to approach the Bigger Brain way of being. We develop more of a relationship with the Universe as the relationships with childish fears and pointless desires fade through our awareness and rejection of them.

It seems that breaking this desire/thought/action chain may be where the Nuns and Monks here do some of their most amazing work. It is a very important reason why they are who they are. Thoughts will pop up, of course. Even highly skilled Wisdom Professionals experience them. But conscious decisions can prevent substandard actions from following substandard thoughts. Again, this happens by being aware enough of the thought to avoid becoming attached to it, controlled by it, fearful of it, or repulsed from it.

As a byproduct of this practice and process, a more positive and constructive interpersonal magnetism is unleashed. Other folks who are also doing things on purpose are drawn to us, and we to them. If we are personally restructuring our experiences toward a more friendly and inclusive way of living, we will find ourselves more often among other people who are purposely restructuring their experiences into more friendly ways of living.

Things generally work out better for people who stay awake enough to pull their own strings. There are fewer reasons to get stressed and aggravated. There is less of the dangerous frustration that comes from life being out of one's own conscious control. We are happy and end up surrounding ourselves with others who are happy. Charisma happens.

We know that it takes work to suffer and it takes work to be happy. Anyone should easily be able to pick the better direction.

In order for any of this work to take place, the mind usually needs to be quiet enough to notice a thought arising in the first place. One has to be able to see a thought clearly and consciously before being able to stop it from becoming an autopilot reaction.

When most folks first try to empty their mind of clutter and chatter, they can't stay on that job for even a minute. Thoughts pop in and out of our little brains as if they had a mind of their own. Recognizing and then gently waving goodbye to unwanted thought as it pops up can be a lot of work, but is certainly doable at a comfortable pace. Little by little it gets easier and easier.

This mind-quieting process reduces stress. If it is causing any stress, a good teacher can help fix that.

Just watch the thought and let it go. Trying to fight it off only attaches you to it as you continue giving that errant thought the attention you don't want to give it.

As a quiet, non-chattering mind is developed, the happy-and-helpful part follows naturally and without much effort. We seem to be nice by nature when we can chip away enough bullshit to uncover that nature.

Nice by nature is where we all come from and where we all want to go. No one is miserable on purpose. Selfishness and misery are mistakes that become habits for some folks, but no one consciously wants to feel like the piece of shit that selfishness and misery make a person feel like.

How can people be selfish and miserable to each other when they believe we all share the same substance, the same humanity, the same Big Brain?

Who would pollute the ocean once they know that *they are* the ocean? Everyone here at the Temple seems to think that the most important thing is every thing, and that life is all about us sharing the Big Brain.

Why don't we teach this kind of stuff in schools?

The popular understanding of reincarnation as rebirth after physical death is also a real consideration among most Nuns and Monks, but it is certainly not the only thing that reincarnation and karma are about.

The "after death" part is not essentially what makes the Nuns and Monks who they are. Making our selves and others happy, while hurting our selves and others as little as possible, is an obvious step in the right direction. This seems to make more sense than haphazardly causing harm but expecting some prepaid version of salvation to defy the immutable law of karma for us in some faraway heaven.

Whatever we do here is what we are most likely to find there.

Some of this information has come from one of the most respected teachers in Honoria. He did not live at our Temple, but his name and ideas are known throughout the country. His name is Buddhadasa Bhikku. If you are interested, more information is available at www.suanmokkh.org.

I would highly suggest going there for the exact facts because, as always, my understanding is filtered through my own little brain. I'm pretty literate and clever for a hitchhiking dog, but I'm no teacher. It is always better to get the bigger picture from someone who uses a bigger percentage of brain. Buddhadasa Bhikku certainly does.

[The word karma that we are familiar with is pronounced *kamma* in Southeast Asia. They use the ancient Pali language in their studies. The more ancient Sanskrit language accounts for the pronunciation of karma or kharma with the "r," as we more often hear it in the West.]

> "When a good deed is done, goodness spontaneously arises; when an evil deed is done, evil spontaneously arises. There is no need to wait for any further results. If there will be any rebirth after death, that rebirth only occurs through the kamma one has done in this very life and the results of which have already occurred here."
>
> Buddhadasa Bhikku, *Kamma in Buddhism*, 2004,
> Parliament of the World's Religions.

*"Our theories of the eternal are as valuable
as are those that a chick which has not yet
broken its way through its shell
might form of the outside world."*

The Dalai Lama

26

The Cat

There's a kennel's worth of dogs here but only one cat. I don't know why and as you know by now, I don't have the language skills to find out.

This cat never left the kitchen during its first month at the Temple. It had that glaze of pain and suffering on its eyes. Most of the skin was missing from one hind leg. It dragged itself around on its forelegs as if it had no hind legs at all. Kitty looked sicker than a crack addict napping on broken glass. My best guess is that a poisonous snake bit it.

My first thought upon meeting the cat was "this poor bastard will be dead within a week," but like everyone else here I tried to do whatever could be done for it. After two weeks of food, petting, and aloe cactus juice on the wounds, the infections went away.

I know what you'd like to hear. I'm sorry that it hasn't happened so far. The cat did not suddenly become fat and healthy with all its legs covered in lustrous fur. It is now over a month later and it still looks injured.

But it looks like it is going to live! Some of the skin and fur have grown back. Kitty walks a bit better and is no longer afraid to leave the kitchen. She survives, perseveres, and makes progress.

Just how crazy is it for an intelligent human being to have a raggedy, poisoned, nearly dead cat for a role model?

Not as crazy as it used to be.

27

Muay Honoria [Honorian Boxing]

I'm from New York City. I've seen some brutal things. I've seen street fights with left-for-dead combatants covered in so much blood that no one could tell if their faces still had noses left on them, or if it mattered any more. I've seen dead heroin addicts the morning after, with skin a mortuary blue color and discharges leaking from every orifice. I've seen bent necks and contorted faces sprawled across vomit-soaked pillows with a "Thank God, it's finally over" look lingering in bleeding eyes, a syringe still clinging to a lifeless arm.

This is all lightweight stuff compared to Honorian boxing. Knees, elbows, feet, and hands are all acceptable lethal tools of destruction. Boxers are permitted to hook their arms behind an opponent's neck and repeatedly ram a knee through that opponent's face or body.

The hardest of bones (the shin) is the most often used part of the fighter's arsenal. It is legal to turn various parts of your opponent to powder with it, whether those parts are above or below the belt. The use of actual weapons in this so-called sport would be an increase in kindness. What cigarettes do to your lungs is the kiss of an angel compared to what Muay Honoria can do to a human body.

It is the Honorian national sport. We have a TV here that is only plugged in for special events. I just watched a couple hours of Muay Honoria with the Monks and Nuns. They love it! Go figure.

28

Brochure, if the Temple Was a Vacation Resort

Private cabin on a hill overlooking virgin beach
Azure ocean within reach
Coconut trees, butterflies, birds
A place where silence hears your words
Caves and jungle on the grounds
Beauty comes here to be found
Warm and friendly native charm
Overt password is "no-harm"
Warm and sunny most of year
Happy fishing village near

Men in orange and gold dress—
everything they touch, they bless.
Women in white *are* compassion—
and cannot be touched by anything but it.

Activities that begin near daylight
stay focused throughout both day and night
on a mental light
that if used quite right
will clear your sight
and increase delight,
bringing remedies to heal your plight
and erase your blight.

Central building is a Temple.
It is also a sanctuary,
an art museum,
and a community center.

Your stay includes a family
that is as concerned about you
as your family back home.

Not everything is perfect.
Perfection, itself, is jealous.

Work hard or sleep long
Enjoy our song and sing along
If you can't sing, we'll teach you
If you desire it, we'll reach you

Donations are accepted
but certainly not required.

Why let your vacation go?
Why not share it here and grow.

29

The Village's People

The village that is adjacent to and governed by this Temple houses about a hundred people. Technically, the people are governed by government, as is true nearly everywhere. But the minds and hearts of this rural population dictate that they live in a theocracy. The Monks and Nuns are authorities. Arjan's word is considered by most folks to be the law. I have seen disputes among villagers decided by our Head Monk. These same disputes would have gone to a courtroom or battleground in the western part of the world.

One small family in this village owns a construction company with contracts all over the province. They are quite wealthy themselves and employ about a dozen neighbors. A few folks here make their living by working in the tourist resorts twenty miles down the road, but most would rather stay home in the village. Most villagers make their living by farming, fishing, or raising cattle. They subsidize minimal incomes with free coconuts and the roots, grasses, and other edible vegetation that grows on the hillsides. Many of my neighbors live in much the same way as their ancestors did a thousand years or more ago.

Even the poorest of this village's people share whatever they have. They give with gratitude as much as generosity, happy for the opportunity to help. A feeling of deep wealth happens here without a lot of material goods—or the concern for them.

Simplicity is a treasured blessing.

Respect is a way of life.

The most impressive part of this village's character is that respect for everything. The same families have been on this plot of earth for longer than legend, but the deep sense of family and community extends beyond the interdependent group of a hundred or so humans. It includes everything natural upon which they depend. There is no human survival without an all-inclusive mutual cooperation between humans and humans, humans and nature, humans and animals, humans and gods.

The idea that cooperation is more important than competition defines this village. There is no benefit to competition in a place where anyone's benefit is effectively everyone's benefit. The village operates as a singular living organism.

The Village Folks at the Temple

The Village Elder

Village women cooking for volunteer workers

Village resident helping to build cabins for Monks

The Village's Traditional Musicians

Drums, the major traditional instrument

Men and women take equal part in the production of music

Mentholated powder helping to fight the humidity

32

The Monk Who Is Not a Monk

Arjan calls my best friend Sepp "the Monk who is not a Monk." Sepp is a forty year old German expatriate and the manager of the Baan Rim Haad Resort. This resort sits about twenty miles down the beach from the Temple. Sepp receives no money for his full time managerial work. He does it because he likes the owners of the resort and the guests that this place attracts.

Sepp was raised in a Bavarian town, eldest son of a family that owned a successful brewery. By the age of twenty five, he had enough money in the bank to retire. Some rich people live in fear of losing what they have. They hoard wealth as a form of combat against insecurity. It often brings them nothing but a materially satisfied misery. Other rich folks have all the confidence and generosity of someone who can afford it. They know they have a privileged life and are grateful for it. An inner security allows them a luxurious quantity of stability that sponsors fearless decency. Sepp is a member of this group.

He is also the person who brought me to the Temple.

Sepp had a serious betrayal experience several years before mine. He lost a lot more than I did. A family that owned a small tourist resort in a neighboring town befriended him. Sepp lived with and worked for them for a year, attracting European tourists and helping the Honorian family run their resort in a European-friendly way. He was responsible for tripling the profits of the family's business. He received no pay, but didn't care. He was already rich, happy enough, and in love with the family's daughter.

My friend didn't know that the daughter was part of the family's plan to get rich by draining an unsuspecting foreigner. These local entrepreneurs had hatched their plan years earlier. They had been waiting for a man who fit the job description to come along. Sepp fit the bill perfectly as a Caucasian with a lot of money who was generous, big hearted, hard working, trusting, romantic, and innocent. He also drank enough to kill a few normal people. This sometimes blurred his judgment more than a bit.

Sepp had increased the Honorian family's business to the point where expansion became necessary. More tourists were showing up than they could handle. These tourists often requested modern conveniences and attractions (air conditioners, swimming pool, better beer refrigeration, modernized rooms, and more). The family hadn't enough money to install the necessary facilities.

During one of Sepp's very infrequent romantic interludes with the daughter, her pillow talk included a request. She wanted a large loan for her family to do the expansion. The understanding was that the expansion of facilities would provide enough increase in profits to insure repayment of the loan. Sepp, as unofficial manager of the place, knew the idea would work.

Had it been a real plan, it would have been a good one. It was not. As soon as a large amount of Sepp's money was transferred into the family's account, they thanked him, asked him to leave, and called the local authorities to ensure his departure. The family claimed that the money was a gift, not a loan. Sepp had no way of proving otherwise. He had no legal recourse. To add insult to injury, the family that stole it gave a cut of Sepp's money to a government official. This ensured that no problems befell the family of thieves. The woman Sepp hoped to marry and the family he thought would become his in-laws had effectively pirated my friend on dry land.

Sepp barely ate and he drank even more heavily than usual for almost a year. He lost a hundred of his former two hundred pounds of body weight.

Sepp recovered from his slow attempt at suicide years ago. As he describes it, "I decided one day, for no apparent reason, that being happy was the only option." He has stuck with that decision ever since.

Sepp doesn't smoke anything, eats as little as any Monk or Nun, and has very little concern for sex. (He does still like his beer a lot.) He is one of the friendliest and most generous people ever born. Anyone who knows him has a great respect for his plainly recognizable strength of character and unassuming righteousness. Sepp has returned from the dead and overcome all bitterness to become a true example of kindness, disguised in humility as a good natured beer hall personality. The bad aspect of self-centered can't find him, while the strength of being a centered-self stays very much rooted in him.

Sepp refers to everyone as "sisters and brothers," and he means it. He is consistently kind to people in speech and action. He has earned the right to speak in brother/sister terms. The man is still too drunk too often. People buy him beers as often as they see him. Sepp never met a beer he didn't like, and I've never met anyone who didn't like Sepp.

Sepp and Tu, whose family owns the Baan Rim Haad resort

Sepp

Sepp's Day Off

Each morning after, I swoon, wheeze, and cough, but I still never miss my best friend Sepp's day off. He cooks, drives, and manages—keeps his week tight, but when Sepp has a day off he sure does it right. We go out together, proceed to get plastered, and when we are done we are two drunken bastards. It's rarely just us two. Folks always come 'round to see what ole Sepp's gonna do to the town.

They come from next door and from miles far away. They know on Sepp's day off that it's time to play. There is no one in this land, I would have to bet, who hasn't had fun at ol' Sepp's day off yet. Elvis and Janis had parties galore, but compared to Sepp's day off they were prob'ly a bore.

Sing into microphones, crank calls on telephones, trek through the jungle to a winemaking uncle, then off to the ocean—perpetual motion! Another good notion! Rub women with lotion!

Sometimes I just stand there and laugh while I'm pissing. If you've not seen Sepp's day off, you don't know what you're missing.

The Recovery from Sepp's day off

34

My Day Off

I follow the rules while on Temple grounds. No drinking, no sex, etc. I try to speak the few words of Honorian I can pronounce, meditate a bit, do my best to control alternative urges, and remember Arjan's main instruction to me: "Make yourself comfortable."

My Master Teacher really is one. He knows that I'm a good man but not at all acclimated to what has become of my own life. He bucks the traditionalists by allowing me to both live at the Temple and go out to get wild before I crack up from various forms of culture shock. This is a very avant-garde situation for a head Monk to allow, but it makes a lot of sense. Neither he nor the Buddha wants me to crack. They've seen that already.

During my first month here, I would turn into a different person when I took the white suit off and left the Temple grounds. I became a vagabond, penniless berserker-on-a-beach-trip who would drink anything with alcohol content and wink at anything female. Luckily, my friends were generous enough to finance some beer. Even more luckily, life always got drunkenly happy enough for me to forget about sex. There's no chance of finding an actual woman now. The word is out that I'm financially challenged. Women want a moneyless, aging man about as much as I want to be soaked in blood and dropped in a pool of sharks.

No problem.

I become a funny person. It works well. Laughter is the best medicine, as they say. Brain tangles release as comedy and everyone's glad I'm around as the jokes flow through the party. When people are glad you showed up, it can make you want to live. If they think you are OK, maybe you are.

This is a shallow, often inaccurate view and not as durable as real internal strength, but a person on the edge will grab onto whatever works. Sometimes it's good enough to just keep living and make progress by the ounce instead of getting frustrated trying to make it by the pound.

Arjan's program is working. By now I'm going out less and the road episodes are milder. I may be losing my taste for the alcohol and getting less shallow too. It is easy to see how Arjan is truly a Master Teacher. He knows how to let things happen. He knows that some things need to fix themselves.

35

Mrs. Jeng's Magic Soup

Mrs. Jeng has a shop in the small town past Sepp's place. She serves up great noodles and soup. There's magic in Jeng and whatever she cooks. It cures all from depression to croup.

If you're sad or you're sneezing, or coughing, or wheezing—no matter what is your malaise—she can fix up your heart or any body part, and remove all your gout, doubt, and daze. It's partly the herbs and partly the spices, and other fine flavorings too. But it's mostly the glow that beams from Mrs. Jeng that helps fix up a cold or the blues.

If I cannot recover from a cold-hearted lover or I catch other chills in my chest, I get feet on the ground and beat them into town. Mrs. J will take care of the rest. When I have hangovers that feel like the plague, one remedy keeps them in tow. Mrs. Jeng fixes up miracles in a cup so that I can get on with the show.

If you've got the feeling you're rocking and reeling and things have gone out of control; if you're feeling sick, your problems are thick, and your life has become a black hole; then try this elixir, it's damn sure a fixer that will give your illness the chase. You'll smile back to the street and your fine dancing feet will surely be back on their pace.

I live in a Temple and don't get to town much—but when I occasionally droop, I quick hit the road and prevent an implode by drinking Ms. Jeng's magic soup.

The Big Brain Version of Magic Soup

Good wishes are pointed at everyone who walks into or even walks by her shop.

Her cooking contains the essence of a prayer on your behalf. Spirit and substance blend in a bowl of blessings.

Mrs. Jeng's good nature is immortal. Hers is a strong and beneficent character. With a concern for you that honestly matches her concern for her self, she floats her comforting demeanor into yours. She relays her personal assurance that everything in the world is fine—just the way it is.

A new customer comes in. Jeng's empathy adjusts to take in and be taken in by him while remaining entrained with all present. That empathy is a jigsaw puzzle that keeps reconstructing its own pieces according to the needs of its background. Jeng grasps new ones as she releases old pieces. She never ceases to amaze herself with stability and a lack of surprise as all these changes take place before her eyes. She is never taken aback by the incredible variety of human emotions that can fit in one small dining room, or within one little person. She thrives on how quickly a person can be coaxed from depths to heights.

Mrs. Jeng knows how to attach both roots and wings to flavor, nutrition, and food-as-medicine. What customers can't see, they can still taste.

Her measuring cups meter volumes of joyful existence as Jeng's resistance to any negative insistence does not run and needn't fight. Negativity dissolves as it runs toward her. She just holds her position and blesses opposition with a wish for a better tomorrow. From the great heart within her, she lets everyone borrow.

Jeng is usually so involved with and concerned for a customer or neighbor that her personal existence takes a back seat. This makes her bliss indestructible. What has donated its substance cannot be hurt.

Describing Mrs. Jeng and why her soup works so well holds the same limitations as speaking about silence.

Mrs. Jeng

37

Bet More

Arjan is the adhesive that holds the whole Temple-and-village unit together, but Bet is the glue that cements local happiness. Sadness runs when it sees him, like a poodle sighting the same German Shepherd that bit him in the nuts yesterday. Bad analogy. Bet will strongly defend his happiness but would never treat anything that harshly. Visiting troubles do leave his presence quickly, but not because he has attacked them. It's more like he buys them a cup of coffee and gives them a ride to the bus stop.

Monk Bet is a Master Electrician in both the physical and metaphysical senses. If a light goes out or a pump stops, he gets it working again.

All of the Temple's residents do some kind of work on the grounds. Some do more while Arjan is around so "the boss" knows they're doing it. I like to do more when he's not around, just to prove to myself that I'm not working to impress him or anyone else. Bet is way past all this nonsense. He wouldn't care whether a mangy dog or Buddha himself was watching. Monk Bet is going to be his happy, helpful self—all day, all week, all the time.

Bet entered life with some advantages. He was born and raised in this village. The man who I think of as a father is Bet's uncle in real life. Bet had a good start.

But just starting well doesn't get you there. Even with the best of starts many people dissipate, lose focus, deny their potential, and turn to garbage. It takes a lot of work and consistent practice to cement a good start into sustained function. Bet obviously has done and continues to do the work. Controlling what one pays attention to has some amazing benefits and implications.

It shocks me to realize that I could be as happy as Bet. Everyone has the ability to grow up. We all have the imaginative facility to reconstruct our lives. We decide what we want the content of our minds, and our lives, to be. All it takes is to be more like Bet, to put some effort, each and every day, into being and feeling better.

What are you doing today? How about tomorrow?

Bet asks me these questions every day without ever saying a word.

Monk Bet at work

38

Sex/No Sex

Right near the top of my list of favorite things to do is sex.

Right near the top of the list of things you can't do on the Temple grounds is sex.

No problem.

According to the Temple's spiritual and philosophical logic, having no sex can be more similar to having sex than one might think possible. A recent conversation with an old European man who rents young Honorian girls brought that last peculiar sentence to mind.

The old man spoke of the Temple residents as if they had psychological problems that were responsible for their lack of sexual activity. He couldn't understand that they had made a conscious, logical decision as to how and where they wanted to direct their energies.

Many people have described the spiritual qualities of sex and orgasm. Doctor Chopra listed several. The spiritual qualities of sex and orgasm include lack of self-absorption, unity consciousness, intimacy, devotion, and a lot of other good things.

Celibate Monks and Nuns sublimate sexual energy and transmute it into positive focus on The Big Brain Thing. They are having some very similar feelings to the ones folks have when getting laid. Let me correct myself. They are having some very similar feelings to the feelings folks have when making love.

OK, even I'm not crazy enough to say there's no difference, but there are some very meaningful similarities as well.

I was going to ask the old man why he thought his habituation to teen prostitutes was superior to the nonsexual ways of the Monks and Nuns, but I'd already heard enough bullshit for one day. I let our conversation die and went on my way.

39

Language Learning

Honorian is a very difficult language for a Westerner to learn, but trying has suddenly become fun. I never put any effort into learning the language during my first year in this country. At first it seemed so strange and difficult that there was no grasping it. After a few months I picked up bits and pieces—a word here, a phrase there. That's when the wife-to-be came on the scene. She spoke English fairly well but wouldn't teach me Honorian, and made sure no one else dared teach me either. It suited her goals perfectly for me to not understand what she was saying to her friends.

By the time the marriage fiasco was finished I'd had enough of Asia, its languages, and life in general. It is hard to learn something when you don't give a fuck about anything.

Leaving the country and not bothering with its language seemed the next logical step. Sometimes while relocating physically a person's mind comes along for the ride, but this was not to be. By the time I figured out that leaving was the thing to do, I was no longer capable enough to hit the road. There wasn't enough money for an airplane ticket, and even with a million dollars I'd have been too psychotic to find the airport. The trip didn't materialize but neither did any further study of the Honorian language. Just as well. It can be uncomfortable and dangerous to travel when you've lost your mind. It is also hard to learn a very foreign language without it.

Things change. I've been in the Temple for a few months now, surrounded by the likes of Arjan, Bet, and Kumnung. These people literally live to help. They think that helping others brings them higher consciousness. I'm starting to believe them.

Having teachers with this attitude makes learning anything a lot more fun. Much unlike the language itself, my ex-wife, or myself, these people are not out to be difficult, take me for an expensive ride, or kill me.

A pleasant surprise has graced my recent study. It seems that during the past year I accidentally picked up about a hundred words, just by coincidental exposure. In the Honorian language one word can sometimes cover ten meanings, depending on the context of the sentence and the inflection of the pronunciation. A hundred words can go a long way.

There is no danger that overconfidence in my Honorian speaking ability will become a problem. As with so many things, it is obvious that there is still a long, long way to go and a lot to learn.

But wanting to do it, as opposed to just wanting to have it done, has already shown advantages. I can now take part in a few mini-conversations.

Thanks to the family, a little progress has been made.

40

Monk Ahn

Writing about the Monks and Nuns gets redundant in a good way. Although they do each have strong, specific individual character traits, there is that consistent underlying similarity that comes from them all being plugged into the same generator and from each one being so aware of that connection.

It is, nonetheless, impossible to get tired of writing about or being with them. These people live as such a friendly prototype of humanity, with so little greed, hate, or selfishness in their makeup, that it is hard to overdose on them.

Monk Ahn would rate near the top of anyone's list of people-we'd-do-well-to-pay-attention-to. Ahn is one of the most friendly and extroverted people on the planet. Like so many of the people here, he defines the concept of being comfortable in one's own skin. His warmth was largely responsible for my quickly believing the truth in Arjan's advice to "think of us as your family now."

No adoption agency in the world has ever done a better placement.

Monk Ahn

41

Chanting, Breathing, Meditation

Ancient incantations provide psychic transportation to a place that is both path and destination. These incantations combine with patience and consistency to nourish every journey, even on the most difficult of roads.

There is no past or future here, only security in the present tense. No tension. There is no danger from any previous trip or the next one while on this voyage. *All* of you is on this singularly directed road.

Rhythmic musical designs jumpstart primeval forces. Ancient wisdoms resurface daily, cementing intelligence to itself.

Warm and safe from interferences, the mind builds tools for clearances of obstacles that are then erased from history.

It's no mystery!

It is a well known path shared by millions before you who have passed out of life but come back to adore you, when you're chanting.

Perseverance required.

42

Meditation, Chanting, Breathing

We *each* own the only key to the door that grants entrance to mind, entrance to thoughts that are coarse or kind. We also own the door. It is our house. No one, no thing, can enter without our permission. Vigilance and diligent practice are locksmiths. Our house is not secure without these.

While experiencing meditation's medication, limitless expanses of Universe meet molecular particles seamlessly, and seemingly endlessly.

Though we are printed on so many pages and grow through a million stages, we are a single entity disguised as uncountable faces and places.

Each face and place is well equipped through a series of graces to maximize function in spaces that range from broad stars to mere atomic traces.

All of us are within each one of us.

The sensations of hearing color and touching sound abound. The most touching sounds trip emotional triggers earlessly. They fearlessly anchor an eerie yet centering effect, as all selves connect in unity, traversing dimensions with impunity.

Meditation's maximum effect abides where *all* secrets reside—in the breath. If you want your body and mind to meet, proper breathing's what you need to repeat.

43

Breathing, Meditation, Chanting

Breathe like a baby. You will hear the wordless lullaby of a mother's rocking arms. Babies know love from both personal mom's and Universal Mother's charms.

Focus on breathing as if there is nothing else to do. Sit still for long enough—*the air will breathe you.* Sit silently. Become the breath. Fill the lungs to their greatest depth. To sit longer is to become stronger.

When breath hears its own heartbeat we find something rare, as life becomes aware of the care we are giving it. This beat cannot come apart. This heart cannot be broken. There will be no breaking in the rhythm it is taking from your making of effort on its behalf.

Internal calm sees external obstacles as dissolving pollution. Dismay finds absolution as the breath rides its wealth to the perfect self that has always been waiting upon our shelf. What wealth is uncovered when instincts are mothered back into existence! No stressful resistance to evil is required once the strength of that evil is disarmed and denied by the flow of the life force (balanced inward and out) to the place where a nest egg of harmonies shout to become you—again. How odd that so many of our confusions can find their corrections, find their solutions, in the simplest and most basic concept since death, in the sweet loving flow of a young baby's breath.

Watching a baby breathe can teach us how to be an adult. Not sucking in or pushing out but balanced and flowing, constantly growing in levels of knowing grace. Knowing *grace* is in the place that it is supposed to be—inside of you, and inside of me.

44

Brothers

Monks Ahn and Chaiyote carrying water past my cabin to theirs

Monk Bet telling me to listen

A rare soccer game with the "summer camp" kids

Monk Mee and Monk Chaiyote looking at my tape recorder

Monk Bet and Me

A child becomes a temporary Monk during summer vacation

Monk Mee and me at the tea station

45

The Temple

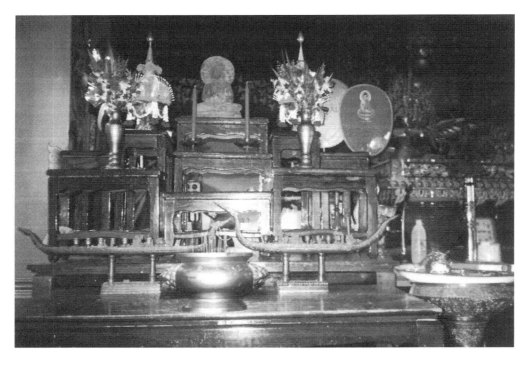

The Sing Along Section

That was a long and heavy chapter!

Let's lighten up a little before getting back to the story.

Reincarnation Through Common Sense was originally a short collection of song lyrics and a serious poem or two. Many of the tune lyrics that follow and a good deal of what is now Section Two composed the collection. It was titled *Temple Songs* and I sold it for two packs of cigarettes to the rare tourists that visited the Temple. Some were impressed in a positive way. It made others dizzy and sick. Several folks laughed hysterically. One woman threw up. They were all probably expecting something more cliché-cosmic and subdued from a Temple dweller in a white suit.

Here, for better or worse, is the original writing and a bit more.

You'll really enjoy many of these a lot more if you sing along with them in your mind, rather than read. Most were meant to be tunes, not poems.

46

Feeding Chilis to Dogs

PRELUDE: *Buddhism is very kind to animals. The dogs at this Southeast Asian Temple get treated better than most humans in any country. We comb through their fur to pick ticks and burdocks off them. They get petted, played with, and loved about as often as they want to be.*

At noon, when the Monks and Nuns are finished eating for the day, the dogs get a large amount of leftovers. They eat the same white rice soaked in a variety of delicacies as the people eat. More often than not, the delicacies contain meat or seafood. These delicious dishes are prepared with the Monks and Nuns in mind, but the villagers know full well that the dogs are part of our community and will be finishing these offerings.

Many of these dishes are spicy enough to scare even the most hardcore lovers of hot food. The dogs get everything, chili peppers included. That brought this little ditty to mind. I picture it being sung in harmony, barbershop quartet style, by four or five dogs with indigestion, ranging from puppy to old age. It could be sung in any number of different rhythms. Pick one you like.

You comb us and feed us, you love and debreed us
if we have the worms in our stool
You let us roam 'round as we damn well please
You pet us and think that we're cool
Your kindness unbounded keeps us hounds unhounded
We're comfy as bumps upon logs
But for the canine life of me I just can't see why you feed
     fucking chilis to dogs

CHORUS
Chili peppers to dogs, chili peppers to dogs
You know we eat a fast bowl
It tears us a new asshole
Buddha answer our prayer or an ulcer we'll share
'Cause you feed chili peppers to dogs

Our coats are all shiny, they glow as if waxed
There are bones in the meat and we love you for that
Our whole lives are blessings, we never get taxed
You give us fine pork, never trimming the fat

Weeeeeee Looooooove Faaaaaaaaaaaaat !!!

We're gratefully not in the streets getting kicked
or born down in India to destitute lepers
But our butts always bleed and we're dizzy and sick
Please give us the food, but hold out the peppers

Chili peppers to dogs, chili peppers to dogs
You know we eat a fast bowl
It tears us a new asshole
Buddha answer our prayer or an ulcer we'll share
When you feed chili peppers to dogs

Note: Truthfully, the dogs are well adapted to the lifelong consumption of these chilis. The spiciness of the food does not bother them at all. If the peppers were disturbing the dogs, the Monks and Nuns would certainly pick them out.

47

Passat Honoria, Poot Mai Dai, Mai Kow Jai
(Language Honoria, Speak No Able, No Understand)

I know it's my fault. I live in your country. I join in your eating and praying.
I listen so hard but it's still no regard. I just don't understand what you're
saying.

I love you and need you, respect you and heed you, and follow wherever
you're going.
But if language were seed, though I water and weed, I still can't get anything
growing.

Your verbs and your adjectives, even your expletives—backwards and all
upside down.
Your alphabet dizzies me, word order frizzies me, gives me an ache in my
crown.

I know you are sweethearts and in my complete heart I feel you are
wonderful folks.
But I can't understand a damn word you are saying. I don't get your songs
or your jokes.

It all seems unpronounceable, tonals denounceable, strangeness imbues
every letter.
I can practice for years—sobered, whiskeyed, or beered—and I don't think
I'd get any better.

Your climate's impressed me and though some things depress me, I love you and don't reprimand.
But the way that you speak sounds like Latin meets Greek. I just can't get the lingo in hand.

Some day the whole world may speak the same language and we will communicate, friend.
But 'til then I must say, though I've tried every way, I just don't understand you (again)!

Mai Kow Jai

48

Farang (Caucasian Alien)

A few of the songs in this collection have multiple meanings or deep universal themes. Some contain venom and others laughter. Most are just fun. None are designed to upset anyone, but a few of them will. My apologies.

You foreign dog, give us your money. Your Nikes stink and your jokes aren't funny. You humped on my sister and called her your honey. Your wealth makes me feel like a half-crippled bunny.

I don't like what you are but still want to be you. Greed is the jailer that never will free you. Don't wait for me to "buddy" or "mate" you. I hate you, berate you—but still imitate you!

You whiskey me, hiss at me, buy up my land. My racism's schism you can't understand. If you disappeared it would surely be grand. But first leave your dollars right here in my hand.

Your TV has swayed me, your manner has played me for the fool that you must think I am. But there's news for you gringo, I'm getting your lingo. I've learned how to cheat, lie, and scam.

Forget about love, it's all about money. Our women are doing their part. We'll feed you and clean you, from cash we'll relieve you as we tear your intentions apart.

We don't even know you. You all look much the same with your pale skin and beady round eyes. We'll hell you and sell you but surely won't tell you all the clever things we have surmised.

After we've drained your cash, stolen soul from its stash, we'll wear your clothes and buy up your cars. Like an Injun in Texas you'll curse us and hex us as we leave you to cry in your bars.

So enjoy your vacation in our scenic nation. We're not jealous 'cause we have it planned. We'll ship your ass out and wave 'bye at the airport, and hope you come back next year, man.

But don't try to stay here, you can't live here all year, you arrogant pasty-faced fuck. We'll carve mind to the bone and then leave you alone where you surely will run out of luck.

Don't whine you white bastard. It couldn't have lasted. There's no sense to make a big fuss.

For our grand final trick (this should finish you, prick!), we'll become you and you'll become us!

49

You Can Only Die Once in a While,
You Can Only Die Once at a Time

—a happy country/western song

You can only die once in a while
You can only die once at a time
What I mean here my friend,
Is that when you reach an end
You can find new beginnings sublime

You feel like you're hangin' at the end of your rope
With lovers, or money, or the wrong kind of dope
But there's really nothing that you cannot fix
If you just learn to use these two little tricks
You can only die once at a time (and in a while)

When your sad life explodes in your face
And you are alone and in total disgrace
Show yourself you've got style
It won't hurt more to smile
You can only die once in a while (and at a time)

You may think it's not worth the trouble no more
Death knocks and you want to open the door
The heat that you've taken has you burnt to the core
And it ain't worth the effort to get up off the floooooor
Buuuuut Reee-memmm-berrrrr

You can only die once at a time
You can only die once in a while
If you stay in the fight
It will turn out alright
And you'll soon have big reasons to smile
Beeeeeeecauuuuuuuuse,
       you can only die once in a while (and at a time)

50

The Temple Crew

—a funky beat tune

There's a crew at the Temple that doesn't wear robes
Though they surely have hearts fit to do it
They know how to relight human flames that flicker
And help those in trouble get through it

Mr. Lee is an artist who can capture a spirit
Right on the end of his brush
He treats humans and canvas with total attention
And can heal with a visual touch

Tae's got laughter and sun in her smile
She's happy as a honeymoon bed
If your heart has sad in it, be with her a minute
All your sorrow will run off in dread

Pookan is a child who is wise past her years
A sage disguised as a young girl
Her eyes speak of warmth and glowing compassion
Shells shatter around this fine pearl

There are several more who can fix a door,
get rid of the ants, or water the plants
Such folks are the grace that makes life seem immense
Pain runs away when it faces their presence

My rhyme may be off but what I know is not
These friends each remember great things I forgot
Sometimes I don't think it's worth spending the day
Until Tae, Lee, and Pookan remind me to play

You're blessed though you're beat and your head's up your ass,
If you've friends who remind you that troubles will pass.

Mr. Lee and Tae in front, their daughter Pookan in the background
(Mr. Lee did the Temple's artwork, featured a few pages ago.)

51

Bored with the Buddha
(I Know the Buddha's Really Bored With Me)

—a standard 12 bar blues tune

I feel like I'm bored with the Buddha
I know the Buddha's really bored with me
Oh yeah, I am bored with the Buddha
No, I think the Buddha's really bored with me

He tells me "just open yo' eyes up"
When I ask for his help to see

Feels like I'm bored with the Buddha
He's heard my whole story before
Now my Temple key is rusty
I can't get in or out the door

CHORUS
(He tells me)
When you finish you're back where you started
When your mind's gone it's still where it's at
I ain't no one who can fix your figure
What you eat makes you skinny or fat!

Oooh I'm gonna stay up on this Temple hill
And I really don't know how loooooooong
'Cause you people did something the Buddha won't do
He'd never try to steal my song

CHORUS
(Still he tells me)
When you finish you're back where you started
When your mind's gone it's still where it's at
I ain't no one who can fix your figure
What you eat makes you skinny or fat!

Ooooh Yeeaaah I feeeeel like-I'm-bored-with-the-Buddha
But I know the Buddha's really bored with me
Guess I'll cue up some Ray Charles music
And hope Other Genius sets me free

52

It's Not That I Won't, I Just Can't

PRELUDE: Pain is personal. It is often hard to communicate to others just how mild or intense your own pain is. Without being able to speak the language, it is very hard to tell my hosts that I am affected by arthritis to a degree that is not always obvious to others. Most folks over here are reasonably fit and work hard into their later years, if they live that long. It is difficult, even for my very sympathetic Temple mates and especially for the villagers, to understand how a person with my apparent largeness and strength cannot perform what they consider very simple tasks. It would be wonderful to clearly explain to everyone that I never want to refuse an invitation, but am sometimes physically incapable of accepting them.

My ankle's been broken, my knees are shot too
I smoke brown cigarettes that turn white people blue
You may not believe me, but I know it's true that
It's not that I won't, I just can't

Indigenous squat
Climb a tree—hey why not?
With no sleep take a trot
Friend believe me it's not
      that I won't, I just can't

Hauling gallons of water uphill
Sit cross legged for Buddha's sweet drill
Soundly sleep while all covered in ants
Find a pocket in pocketless pants
Carry logs, start a fire
In a wet monsoon mire
Dig a hole, plant a plant
Mind desires—body can't
It's not
      that I won't I just can't!

You're On Your Own

—an illegally medicated ballad

You may have Mapmakers and Great Master Teachers
Be in touch with Great Spirits and Galaxy Reachers
A great mate, great friends, and a fancy cell phone
But whatever you have, you are still on your own

You may have a great psychic sense of direction
It won't help if you make even one wrong selection
Of a path, friend, an atmosphere, lover, or home
When you make your decisions, you make them alone

Some days you'll pick brilliant, some days you'll pick dark
Walk on broken glass or a walk in the park
Only you do the picking. You know, if you're grown
That whatever you figured, it was done on your own

Peace? Love? War? Hate?
Find a partner? Masturbate?

I'm not being sarcastic. I'm not being cynical
This is so consistent that it's near textbook clinical
You'll find when you reap, it's from seeds that *you*'ve sown
Steering life wisely is a good skill to hone

Yew Jus' Canned Dew Nuthin Aboud It

—a way, way backwoods yahooin' hillbilly country tune

It's open mike night at the trailer park! Send the teenage girls off to Gramma's house
and then lock up the medicine and gun cabinets before the cousins get here!

You just can't do nuthin about it,
no you can't do nuthin at all
Your kids are half crazed, your wife's always dazed
And you're so drunk you piss in the hall
No you can't do nuthin at all

Well you just can't do nuthin aboud it,
So you might's well go have you some fun
What the heck, you redneck, go and shuffle your deck
Just remember to lock up the gun
Go get neked and lay in the sun

You ain't got the dime to take the trolley to town
You're pissin clear, the tap water is brown
Half your life's spent lookin up from the ground
Your friends all agree (though they're never around)

That you just can't do nuthin aboud it,
no you can't do a damn thing at all
Life's dealt you these cards, and though it may be hard
You still have to answer the call
Oh! And you cannot change that at all

Sometimes I just set here a laughin,
'bout the good times and bad times and such
I don't really care if Miss Perfect ain't there,
I can always find somethin to touch

Gonna laugh, sing, and dance at my funeral,
although I will not really be there
"Can't do nuthin aboud it,"
yep, I'll be there to shout it.
If the mourners all faint, I don't care!

55

My Special Song, Just for You

And now I'd like to do a special song just for you. What key is it in?

The Next Year/The Next Song

May the next song you write be your greatest
May the next year you have be your best
May the next thing you think make you happy
And may God take you unto her breast

May the next book you read make you smarter
May you always be lucky in love
May you never feel used, like a martyr
What you hope for, may you gain above

May whatever your next aspiration
Be granted immediately
May the things that you need and the effort you breed
Always coincide successfully

May the troubles you feel are impending
Be released in the flash of an eye
And whatever you define the terms as
May you always be happy and high

May your pain be unable to find you
May you always have a hand to hold
And if life gives you anything evil
May it soon be turned back into gold

'Cause your next song is always your greatest
And your next year is always your best
And if you feel like this, life will give you a kiss
And your living will always be blessed

56

Deeper Freedom (versus Criminal Mischief)

This one may be a bit hard for many older folks to sing along with, but for anyone who can handle a hip-hop/rap beat, it is doable.

It is time to unhinge from what hell always tells us—that no one can be well most of the time, in flow with their rhythm, in step with their rhyme.

Trauma and drama *are not* every day things that must be accepted as life clips our wings. Freedom from anger and confusion becomes a full time mental resident as we wave goodbye to false evidence and climb the fence that had us locked out and blocked off from happiness. Now free of the lies and bad news that we learned, it is easy to see how barbarians burned us by twisting our history for their selfish purpose, without any regard for truth or good service.

How much of our lives is a bad figment of someone else's imagination?
Who is in charge?
Why don't they do a better job?
What stops us from stopping them?
How did it get so bad and go on so long?
It doesn't matter. Bygones, by definition, are gone.

Here in the present tense, some issues need to be addressed.

Why settle for less than being your best? Even when we can't improve what life gives, we can always improve how we deal with it. Yes, of course, there is some earthly action that is beyond our hold but a much bigger fraction is within our control. We can timidly cower when shit hits the fan, or fan out our feathers and make a strong stand. To choose a direction with courageous inflection is our greatest power, if we rise to the hour.

Freedom from basic tweaking isn't basic for everyone. Some people get warped and stay bent, ignoring great opportunities to reinvent themselves. Choosing wiser ways up can prevent the fall down (keeping head in the sky, but feet on the ground). It is always our own choice to wear horns or the crown.

Everyone seems to think that the way they feel is what defines "real." What does the word "real" really mean? Responses to this question include brilliant profanity, range from joy to insanity, from serious and weighty to flat out inanity. Answers fall in line according to who is seeing the "real," and what they have seen of "real" in the past. "Real" moves around and can change very fast. As illusory imprints get remembered and last, the facts all too often get passed to oblivion. With truth in oblivion, our entire criterion for judging anything becomes suspect. "Real" can inspire anything from passive receptivity to manic activity.

It can be frustrating and confusing when you seem to be losing all familiar reference points. Defensive fear can steer anyone near to the far edge of sanity, if we believe that selfish inanity is the core around which humanity is based.

No, you lying bastards! I'm not going to get the girl if I buy your cologne, or car, or whatever else you are selling. There's no telling how many people are smelling your cologne at home alone while you are making love to the profits you've stolen from their dreams. How many times have you killed the trust they paid for? Now only those who think they have nothing left to lose can afford trust. Too much of so-called "reality" is commercial greed that likes to feed on the programmed need of its victims.

Not me! I'm relaxed. I'll no longer be grinding my ax because someone else makes up my facts. Everyone knows by now that facts don't always tell the truth. Ask the average citizen in a voting booth! But frustration and anger only hurt the self. They rarely give us what we could call help. Even righteous indignation isn't righteous anymore. There is no time, good purpose, or need to plant seed that can breed even more discontent in this world where the "real" has already been spent.

It is time to repair the unreal in the air.

This seems only fair.

We did put it there.

Deeper freedom insists on taking back all the misused time that can slip through the cracks. Better to taste it than waste it. That time can be used to sit, breathe, and not think. To *not think* is more intoxicating than any drink. It shows the common sense in living immense based on love's recompense, without manic defense caused by fear that's intense.

Deeper insights of a valuable kind arise more easily to the quiet mind.

Freedom doesn't mean everything is perfect. Like it or not, some external things can't be changed. Accepting whatever presents itself and mining it for educational wealth keeps us sane. From each painful stain there is something to gain. What cannot be changed, we must endure. This is a fact of which you can be sure. There are options, but there is no choice. No need for discussion. Save your voice.

People who consistently suffer chains of unfortunate events need to stop being an unfortunate event. Rewards come to those who make effort with care. There's no doubt this will happen if we point toward repair.

Every victim has the freedom to create his or her own immediate reincarnation as a non-victim by keeping the physical body but losing attachment to its negative history. Getting life past the past is what solves that life's mystery.

Patience gives us freedom from a lot of aggravation that affects people who have no patience. The frustration of trying to control things that cannot be controlled ties freedom in knots. Patience can untie those knots and prevent future tangles as it sees other angles.

Happiness, like freedom, attracts itself. It draws together like-minded circumstances and then freely dances in the magnetism that relates them. That magnetism negates isolation through the firm preservation of the union between our selves and others. With strangers, allies, enemies, or brothers this magnetism may vary in style, strength, and duration, but refuses negation of Natural Law's regulation of interdependence under any circumstance.

This magnetism tells of an immortal law that says we, all together, are, at our core, one singular unit of organic humanity. This law carries more weight than the simultaneous fact that we are separate humans doing singular acts. We can admit that this Natural Law rules or deny it like fools. It is as real as gravity. These magnetic forces bind us as a unit while allowing individuality. They tie us together while setting us free.

Treating everyone and ourselves very well is a refusal to enter the gates of those hells that tell the story all too well of the millions of people resigned to a fate that they hate in a world they waste time to berate, instead of making it great through intelligent efforts that they could propagate.

If, with no compromise, we open our eyes to the best possibility in each situation, we then avoid that mental masturbation that informs us that we are bad boys and girls that do not deserve a harmonious world. This aggressively depressive cultural stroking is guilt-fed and regressive. It never ends in a mutually rewarding societal orgasm.

"That's just the way it is" is not a historical given! We manufacture "the way it is" daily. Freedom always allows making changes through choices. Defending this right to make choices is worth our loudest voices.

The present tense is our only true source of sense. It is always here and now. The past is long gone. Future never arrives. Where we are is the only place we live our lives. Deeper freedom evicts historical angers with no more recompense than "goodbye." Why? Because it is true that negative history can block positive mystery. Keeping past in the past, obstacles vanish quickly and the present gets healthy though the history was sickly. Most lacks of deeper freedoms are self-inflicted wounds. Long ago traumas plague folks to their tombs—unless remedied.

External evils cannot get within a comfortable skin. It is my skin, to wear as I please! There will be no submission to evil or sleaze. Nonsense within starts to whither and die. As it all goes by, memories that blocked our great high realize they don't own us. Nice bonus!

The most noticeable thing about deeper versions of freedom is that they are within each individual's command (although other folks can certainly lend us a hand). We shine from our own places as we grow to understand that perfecting our own instrument gets us into the band. Freedom is an inside job, an attitude thing. Each of us chooses which tune we will sing.

Through strength and empathy lives are made great. We've heard the golden rule. We all can relate. Keeping freedoms within the golden rule is the way to insure that life always stays cool. Freedom of speech doesn't allow us to yell "Fire!" in a crowded theater—unless the theater is actually on fire.

Then yelling, "Fire!" becomes a fulfilled obligation, a thing of great beauty, and a sweet civic duty instead of criminal mischief.

Mail to Friends

Writing to you as a friend is what made this a book. If I were just writing stories for myself, or for an audience I pictured as strangers, the book would not have happened.

Thanks for being there.

Here are some conversations we've had.

57

Chad

Most of the folks you meet in Honoria are very pleasant. Honorian natives are notoriously happy people who smile more often than not. Even those with ulterior motives are patient and pleasant while they're screwing you. Those who aren't after what you have are a joy to be with. Most of the foreigners here are vacationing, having fun, and are good company as well.

Every once in a while you meet an asshole.

I was hanging out with my buddy Sepp at his resort's bar. After more than a few beers we were feeling pretty good so the loud, obnoxious man who suddenly appeared uninvited at our table didn't disturb us—at first. The problem wasn't that he invited himself to the table. Almost everyone at a beach resort is on the same buzz and invitations are not usually required. Most travelers are happy and communally welcomed wherever they sit.

There are exceptions.

Chad was one of them. There's no sense in telling you his country of origin. Assholes, like saints, come from everywhere. His voice was screeching chalk across a blackboard. He knew everything and everyone who ever existed anywhere. Whoever he was speaking at was assumed to be too stupid to appreciate the grandeur of his presence, but magnanimous Chad was benevolent and forgiving to his inferiors. He was kind enough to stomach us a bit longer for the purpose of having more time to feed us shit.

In Brooklyn, Chad would've gotten his ass kicked in five minutes or less, but Honoria is more polite than Brooklyn and the resorts have to carry tolerance to an even greater level.

Chad rattled on about all he knew and we did not know, how much he had done that we never would, and the wonderfulness of "The Chadster" and the very few people like him.

I was getting a headache from this prick. I closed my eyes, took a deep breath, and tried to keep my composure intact.

When my eyes opened again, I was on my sleeping mat in the cabin at the Temple. First daylight was coming through the window. Chad had been a dream.

Something was telling me to be very careful about never moving in the direction of Chad-like behavior.

58

Herb

Most of the folks I've met in Honoria have been very pleasant. Honorian natives are notoriously happy people who smile more often than not. Even the few with ulterior motives are patient and pleasant while they're screwing you. Those who aren't after your money are usually a joy to be with. Most of the foreigners here are having fun. They are often good company as well. It is rare to meet someone so exceptionally decent that they shine above even the best of the rest.

Herb was at the bar drinking slowly. We could tell he was not used to vacation quantities of alcohol. Nonetheless, the drunker he got, the more pleasant he seemed to become. Every difficult experience he spoke of was framed in terms of the silver lining around the cloud. He gave details of crimes he had suffered in terms of sympathy for the perpetrator and the conditions that must have led to his abuser's problems. If someone threw a rock at his head, Herb would probably tell us of the inspiring hallucination he had during the concussion and the unfortunate circumstances his poor attacker suffered as a child.

Herb's soft but energetic voice transmitted a calming strength that was as contagious as laughter through a crowd of children. Everyone felt it and was grateful. Folks kept buying him drinks that he obviously didn't need, just so he wouldn't leave.

Herb didn't overdo the horror stories, but we could all tell that he hadn't had an easy life. Some folks are the privileged few. They grow up surrounded by loving kindness in an idyllic environment and it becomes natural for them to grow into good qualities. Herb didn't fit that mold. He worked for every progress he had made. This gave him an added dimension. He had an experiential wisdom to go with his kindness. His eyes afforded anyone looking into them a no-detours trip through hell up to heaven.

After a few hours and several beers with this amazing person I was feeling very good. I closed my eyes and took a deep breath to drink it all in. When my eyes opened, I was on my sleeping mat watching daybreak through my cabin's window at the Temple. Herb had been a dream.

Something was trying to tell me to be very consistent in practicing Herb-like behavior. (Make all the 420 references you like. They'll fit.)

59

Mr. Mee Becomes a Monk

Today my buddy Mr. Mee becomes a Monk. Mee's inspirational example has touched everyone here. He has come such a very long way since leaving the ghetto hell of the capitol city a half year ago. After graduating from stone cold junkie to alcoholic he spent all the rent money drinking, and was then moved into the Temple by his wife Kumnung. He has worked very diligently ever since—spiritually, mentally, and physically.

Mee is completely involved in the effort to improve his own life and the lives around him. He works inwardly, outwardly, and upwardly. His eyes are always on both the process and the prize. He has done a masterful job of realizing that the road *is* the destination, if you keep moving forward on it. Gradually working from degenerative self-involvement to regenerative altruism, he has become a living example of "Anything is possible!" and "Can do!"

We're all very proud of Mee. I hope he stays an inspiration to all of us here, and to himself. The old Honorian expression says that a Monk becomes a Monk *tuk wan* (every day). Without that daily effort, one can reach a plateau and then rest on laurels until talents rust and inspiration goes stale. Mr. Mee won't have that problem. He will remember where he came from.

The process should continue to get easier for Monk Mee from here on. The further up the evolutionary ladder a person climbs, the more he or she will be surrounded by the influence of people who are further up the evolutionary ladder. Those influences will help him.

60

Mr. Mee's Induction Ceremony

Mr. Mee was initiated as Monk Mee in a series of ceremonies. Each ritual became a little more intense than the one before. I missed part one, the head shaving ritual. While the shaving was going on, I was busy making up a gift for my soon-to-be-Monk friend. Gifts are typically money or baskets of food. Most of what any new Monk gets is passed on to his family.

Having no access to food or money, I rummaged through my few possessions hoping to find something suitable. Symbolic bits and pieces had been collecting in my duffle bags for decades. There were a few Mee might appreciate.

A small woven basket came out of the second duffle bag. It had enough room to hold other gifts. I began filling it with talismans, hoping these would symbolize ideas that might help Monk Mee travel his new road. Most of the talismans were collected too long ago for me to remember where they came from, but it was easy to remember why I kept them.

The first item was a paper poppy flower bought in America about two or three wars ago from the Veterans of Foreign Wars organization. It was put in the basket as the first gift. It was meant to reinforce the notion for Mee that he was now an ordained ambassador of peace and nonviolence.

A brown crystal rock fragment, a piece of present day Earth, was included to remind him that this physical earth and its creatures make up our current office. With all due respect to more cosmic concepts of heaven, hell, and other dimensions—we are here right now. This is where and when the job needs to get done.

Fifty Baht ($1.20 US) was also dropped in the basket. It was more than I could really afford. It was entered as a token of my hope for both his personal prosperity and his detachment from concern about it.

A small eraser was included to remind him that no mistake needs to be permanent. This one really wasn't necessary, as Mr. Mee was already a poster boy caliber living example of this notion. I put it in anyway. Just in case he slipped a little in the future, looking at it might quickly remind Mee to erase the problem's cause and not spiral into deeper trouble.

A small Chinese wooden amulet with faded, unreadable symbols painted on it was also included. If the world's most brilliant scholars studied it until the end of time, they could not decipher its mystery. Some things are just like that.

A small painting of a dragon on a block of wood was meant to represent conviction, determination, and strength of heart and mind.

There was a box of matches to remind him that if he ever ran out of light, there was always more available.

Packrats and road residents like myself often find what they need somewhere in their stash. A small piece of wrapping paper and a smaller piece of ribbon surfaced from the far depths of the second duffle bag in honor of the occasion.

I took the gift into the Temple to install some power into each item through focused meditation. The belief around here is that if you put attention into something, even into an inanimate something, that attention will to some degree affect and empower whatever it is being transferred to. It is not just a sweet thought. Putting energy into something seems to work! It is more obviously believable when attention is given to a child, pet, or spouse and it causes them to noticeably perk up. But energy is energy, and giving it seems to make a difference no matter where, when, by whom, or to what it is given.

The usual near-silence of the Temple area was replaced by loud celebration today. About fifty of Mee's friends and relatives were eating, singing, talking, dancing, cheering, and laughing near the windows. It was not a distraction. I was totally and singularly focused on directing attention, good wishes, and potency into the gifts.

In the middle of my process, the back door to the Temple opened and in walked—no, floated—a glowing human creature of indeterminable age or sex. My attention to installing power into the gifts dissolved into awe for this presence. *Who was this?* An outfit of white cloth and gold lace was framed by the brilliant sunshine behind it. The outfit itself framed a person of dark brown skin who seemed to radiate a glow rivaling that of the sun itself. The obvious aura had me wanting to both become part of it and run for sunglasses. My first thought was, "Wow! They must have brought the heavyweights out for this party!"

The figure said "Sa wat dee, kahp!" ("Hello!") to me. His bald head was shining, but not as brightly as the glow around it. With a grace more powerful than is usually contained in any human's walk, he took a few steps toward me, smiled, and said "Kin kao?" ("Have you eaten yet?")

I finally recognized my friend Mr. Mee.

He had just completed the head shaving ritual.

IN OUR TEMPLE

Everyone gathered into the Temple. Our Head Monk and Master Teacher spoke briefly to the crowd.

He then relayed ancient transmissions to Mee.

The "relaying transmissions" thing deserves a little explanation. It seemed that Arjan was doing something in addition to saying prayers and giving blessings. It felt like he was sharing a history as well as transferring an energy and responsibility to Mr. Mee. This did not appear to be the kind of energy transference where something is lost by giving it away. It looked more like a one plus one equals three kind of thing. These same energies may have been shared between senior and novice Monks since ancient times.

Arjan repeated timeless incantations and Mee responded according to the ancient prescriptions. Mee did (almost all of) this appropriately. The initiate was a bit nervous, but anyone going from junkie to alcoholic to hardest working man in a monastery to Monk in less than one year might blow a few lines of the script at his ceremony!

The faces of family and friends displayed the type of pride that is not a sin. It was on my face too.

I thought this was the whole ceremony. It was only the preliminary round!

The crowd packed tightly into pickup trucks and moved to the bigger Temple five miles up the road.

THE MAIN CEREMONY

The air is electrified. Small clusters of folks chat while the elementals of the ceremony gather. Monks from Temples throughout the province have come to take part. Anyone paying attention can feel what is happening. A singular energy is building among these Wisdom Professionals. A unified and unifying force contributes itself to, as well as distributes itself through, the collective of ordained bodies. Each individual is fully present, but individuality takes a back seat. The combined energies of all the Monks gathered and the forces they are beseeching take precedence. It is something like moving a heavy couch with your friends. Individuals put energy into the effort knowing that only the group as a unit can get the job done.

Once the energy has collected, a procession begins. Younger brothers, smiling children, old men and women—no one is left out. The drunk, sober, and joyfully entranced are all out in force. We walk around the Temple three times while screaming, cheering, singing, shouting. The purpose of all this is to scare off any negativity that might create obstacles to the process. It doesn't matter whether that negativity comes from the new Monk's old memories or a stray symbolic demon that was inadvertently brought on the grounds by a member of the crowd. We yell at them all. It feels like someone has beaten us to it. It feels like any obstacles to this process were banished a thousand years ago.

I carry a straw mat.

When the walk ends, Arjan instructs me to lay the mat down in front of the altar at the Temple's entrance. Here Mr. Mee lights candles and incense, and is once again blessed by Arjan. This ritual has all the color, joy, and gravity of a coronation.

Gravity, itself, is about to meet its match.

Once we enter the Temple, the drunken people become sober and very much resemble the smiling children. The atmosphere is ecstasy.

There are eighteen Monks on the stage area. They are a singular unit of positive power and energy joined in an effort to make the nineteenth Monk a reality. They begin chanting with Mee in the center receiving the transmissions. The look on his face is one that I have never seen on a human face before or since. He looks something like a newlywed who is simultaneously at the altar and basking in the afterglow of a very satisfying honeymoon, but with the usual sexual component completely out of the picture.

The "beyond words" cliché fits well in describing the nearly two hours of ceremony. Words can't do justice to the process itself or the psychic byproduct of its performance.

I'll do what I can with it.

This Temple has windows all around it. The light distribution is uniform throughout. It is daytime. The electric lights are off. But there is a very visible brilliance on the stage itself. This is not a symbolic brilliance. It is as obvious as headlights on a car.

The chants and melodies are themselves hypnotic. The varied tones of Arjan, then Mee, and then all the Monks in the chorus trading repetitions and verses are also hypnotic. Is all this more hypnotic to my English-language ears? Without knowing the meaning of the lyrics, do the tune and rhythmic beat of the chants have a deeper impact on me than on the people who can actually follow what is being said? I don't think so. A quick look around the crowd reveals a blessed out, blissed out, otherworldly expression on the face of each and every person in the building.

About an hour into the ceremony, Mr. Mee's mom, his wife Kumnung, and a few other female relatives all start crying at the same time. I know without being told that this part of the ceremony installs Mee as a karmic son of the Buddha. This officially severs his ties and responsibilities as husband to Kumnung, and his role as mother's son, brother to his sister, nephew to his uncles and aunts, and so on.

The ceremony ends and everyone exits the Temple. Only the Monks and Nuns still obviously have their feet on the ground. Everyone else gives the appearance of floating. In less than a minute, those who were the happy drunks turn happily drunk again, as if there were no interruption.

The former Mr. Mee is now officially Monk Mee.

Monk Mee with our Senior Monk

Monk Mee studies

61

Ever Kissed Your Sister?

Mr. Mee is now Monk Mee, and that is a wonderful thing. Kumnung, his lifesaver and wife of eight years, is our Temple's favorite daughter. Her job is done. She will only be with us for one more week. Then Ms. Kumnung will go back to the capitol city and clean fish in the downtown market to support her young son and eighty year old mother. She will face a drastic downturn in lifestyle. She will live in a tin roofed cardboard hut in a nasty slum settlement that is a hotbed of crime and disease.

It was Kumnung who got Mee to where he is today. She stayed with him, helped him, and supported him. He could not have done it without her. Mr. Mee told me this himself. He didn't have to. It has always been obvious.

Mee and Kumnung are no longer married. This was made official during that part of his ordination ceremony where all the women started crying. It is a part of many spiritual traditions worldwide that a person devoting his life to divinity is automatically divested of familial relations and responsibilities.

Mee becoming a Monk is what everybody wanted. Kumnung probably wanted it more than Mee himself! But for every night-before there's a morning-after. It is Kumnung's morning-after now. You can see it in her face. It is as obvious as the sickly green tint of any painful hangover.

She's forty years old, sick, overweight, and nearly as penniless as I am. The hard streets of the capitol city may not recognize this angel who is loved by everyone at the Temple. The steaming pollution of downtown Asia could chew up her happiness, perhaps her life, and spit it into an open sewer without a second thought.

But if there is an ever-operating Law of Karma, Kumnung will be fine. If there is any goodness or decency in the world, harm *cannot* come to this woman.

And there certainly is goodness and decency in the world.

It's in her.

I'd go with her myself, but it would be too much like kissing my sister.

62

The Healers

I've been studying herbal medicine and so-called alternative healing practices for about thirty years. When the healers came to stay at the Temple for a month, my interest was awakened. I'm such a firm believer in natural healing methods that my definition of the drug and surgery dominated modern medical industry is *emergency-only medicine.*

Our modern allopathic medicine seems superior to natural methods only in severe emergencies—or if you want to become a legal drug addict. My personal experiences with more ancient and less invasive techniques include the herbal cure of a liver ailment that modern medicine said would kill me, and a five year release from cigarette addiction through bioelectrical energy healing. I haven't been to what most people call "a regular doctor" for twenty five years.

The healers were scheduled to spend a month with us. Something told me to watch this newly arrived group from a distance. I did. Many folks didn't. Crowds arrived from all over the province and camped by the Temple's entrance.

The spiritual and functional headman of this healing group was about fifty years old, at least thirty pounds overweight, and a very heavy cigarette smoker. The massage and herbal practitioners assisting him were all saintly in demeanor, but each had obviously uncured physical ailments of their own.

The staff's problems notwithstanding, many patients came out of the treatments saying that they had experienced benefits. I saw two different people being carried around by relatives on the first day. By the end of the second week each had taken a few steps by themselves. I communicated with a Monk and a Nun who each had assorted small pains cured in a day.

How much of such cures is faith healing or mind over matter is always a question—but a positive, nontoxic result certainly justifies the means in medicine. The body knows how to help itself if the mind directs it to do so. The infirm will often transfer the authority to facilitate that directing to someone they believe to be more special or more knowledgeable than themselves.

Faith factor aside, there truly are healers who have special training and natural gifts. And there are those who do not.

There were several other facets of the healers' program besides the faith that the ill brought with them. Nutrition, no doubt, played a part. Many people in Honoria survive on white rice and chili peppers. That is not exactly an all-inclusive storehouse of vitamins. The healers and our community provided regular, balanced, and varied meals along with and as part of the treatments. This alone probably cured some ailments on the spot! The healing encampment was a month in culinary paradise for some. Several of the camping faithful may *never* have eaten that well for an entire month in a row.

Massage was also provided. This treatment has a long and well documented history of multiple benefits. The psychological edge of receiving a professional's caring touch, the increased flow of blood and its oxygen to afflicted areas of the body and to the brain, and the dismantling of blockages in the human energetic circuitry are just a few of the perks that have made massage such a widely respected treatment throughout the international history of healing.

Herbal infusions were also used. It is common knowledge that the right herb administered to the right person at the right time can be incredibly effective.

In addition, everyone was getting very well rested and on a Temple's grounds in a very religious society. These folks were not spending their energy on the daily fight for survival, as they usually did. Besides resting their physical bodies, they mentally had time to completely focus upon their health as well as the idea that the Buddha himself wanted them to regain it. There was a lot of prayer, lecturing, and chanting by the headman that served to reinforce these notions.

Our Temple's regular chanting sessions added authenticity to this mix.

The main attraction seemed to be the headman's short personal session with each individual patient. About a hundred people each day took a number and waited in line to spend five minutes getting joked with and spat on by him. He kept the crowd laughing (another well known curative factor). When the laughter lightened a bit he'd get a serious look on his face, chew up some medicinal leaves, and spit the juice on the afflicted part of his patient. It seemed that the herb was thought to be somehow translated into the individual biological language of the patient's need as well as amplified in strength and effect by combining with the energy (and saliva) of the healer. It reminded me of published studies I'd seen about American Medicine Women in Appalachia who can heal tissue damage and lessen the pain of a burn victim just by blowing on the wounded tissue.

My knees are worn, but by now I know enough to tend to myself pretty well. Arjan's shoulder was a little overworked yesterday. I asked if he was going in to get the shoulder worked on by the healers. He replied, "I think I'll fix it myself."

Healers and doctors can be a very helpful (and sometimes essential) part of anyone's life, but nobody knows what things really feel like better than the person who is actually feeling them. In many cases (especially the minor ones) you can be your own best doctor.

Proper and thorough education is definitely required for self-treatment of even the most minor ailments. Proper professionals are almost always required to advise on or treat more serious ones.

63

Honorian Culture and Customs

(for the tourist)

Honorian culture is vastly different from Western culture. Even expatriates who have been here for decades continue to be baffled. The kingdom has never been conquered by a European power. This admirable independence has resulted in a unique culture that can seem somewhat introverted and confusing to visitors.

This is a country of incredible human warmth and natural beauty. It is well worth visiting. Here is a bit of advance information for any of you who may want to avoid some of the social pitfalls and dizzying culture shock during your visit.

Honoria is known as the land of smiles. A smile cast in your direction can mean, "I love you," or "Go fuck yourself," or anything in between. Think and act positively. Most of the smiles shot your way will be genuinely pleasant.

Avoid paying any attention to the word "*farang*." You'll go nuts trying to figure out when it is a harmless, friendly reference or a cutting insult. It is not usually meant to be nasty and can even be a term of endearment.

If you do make a cultural mistake, you will most often be forgiven. Don't worry. Relax. Honorians are aware that their culture is as strange to us as ours is to them. They are very understanding on that account. The only trespasses considered serious are open insults to either the royal family or a person's religion.

Although being forgiven is easy, it is still a very good idea for the visitor to know and observe some of the national customs. This earns you *respect*, which is among the most valuable assets anyone, foreigner or national, can enjoy. This is true worldwide of course, but respect in this nation is one of life's absolutely essential requirements. It is the main building block of Honorian social culture.

Knowing a bit of the language is a major benefit. As in any country, knowing even a few words shows that you've at least made an effort. The natives respect that.

You have no doubt seen the greeting practiced in parts of Asia. Hands joined at the palms with fingers pointing up and held together in front of the body. This is known as the "Wai." Often the head is slightly bowed as a respectful hello or goodbye ("*Sa wat dee, kahp*" in either case) is spoken in conjunction with the Wai.

The Wai is a sign of respect as well as a greeting. There are many stories about its origin. All probably have some degree of truth to them. One says that the greeting was originally meant to show that a person had no weapons in hand and therefore friendly intentions. Another states that it is related to India's "*Namaste*" greeting, which translates as "I see the divine quality within you." This would make sense within the Buddhist framework of this country, the Indian origin of Buddhism, and how close the two countries are geographically located.

The various heights at which one holds the hands in a Wai position do have meaning, but local folks don't expect vacationers to know about this. It's all good, but you'll make an even bigger hit with the natives by remembering the levels of Wai. The palms held at the height of the forehead is usually reserved for greeting ordained folks in robes or royalty. The palms are positioned in front of the nose to address a teacher or someone in a position of authority (or advantage). Palms are held in front of the heart for general use. This is still a very friendly gesture showing respect. Again, don't strain your brain around this one. Honorians don't expect visitors to know it.

You can say "Sa wat dee, kahp" (*kah* instead of *kahp* if you are a woman) to anyone, but never do the Wai to a child unless the child has greeted you with the Wai first. This is a very age conscious culture where elders are given great respect. If you Wai a child first, some locals believe you are treating that child as older. Some are actually superstitious enough to believe that this can steal years from the child's life! Again, don't panic. You will be forgiven quickly but to do a better job of making friends, impressing the natives and respecting your hosts, it will help to remember a few of these cultural idiosyncrasies.

Bottom and top mean a lot in Honorian social structure, as they relate to body parts and other facets of culture. The lowly foot should never approach the more heavenly head. The higher on the body you touch a person, the less polite it is considered. You'll see men patting each other on the ass or holding hands (as opposed to the more Western habit of putting your arm on a buddy's shoulder). It doesn't have anything to do with sexuality. A lower touch is just a friendly gesture showing more respect than a higher touch would. Never pat anyone but a small child on the head. Do not point the bottoms of your feet toward a Monk, Nun, or the altar of a Temple.

The following may be the most important thing to remember.

If you want to look like a total jerk to Honorian people, display anger in public. A very high regard is placed on *staying cool* in all situations. They also frown on positive displays of emotion, so you won't see much hugging or kissing in public either. But if you've got to avoid only one of these, make it the anger and arguing. To these people, yelling at another human in public makes you look like a monkey throwing shit balls. It is also considered a serious insult to the person you are yelling at.

Whether it involves shouting or not, public criticism is considered similar to violence. Honorian people don't have a Western sense of friendly, humorous, or constructive criticism.

Honorians are very clean people who bathe and change clothes often. If you want to make friends with the locals, the laundromat is not the place to make budget cuts.

Throughout much of Asia you can pick your nose in public all day long if you like and no one will care, but it is considered impolite to pick your teeth (with or without toothpick). If you must pick, cover your mouth with the hand that isn't doing the picking.

When a rural Honorian person that you know wants to look in your shopping bag, it is standard procedure and nothing to worry about. They are not trying to steal your stuff. Big stores that put things in bags won't come to the rural villages here for at least another generation or two. In many places, the only things that stick out of a bag are groceries—and each cloth bag is the shopper's personal property. Any resident of a small village returning from a shopping trip to the city would be considered *a happening*. The community, being as closely knit as it is, would be excited to know what novelties their neighbor had brought home from the big city in those fancy plastic bags. That neighbor would be glad to show his purchases to everyone.

Do not, however, go through a Monk or elder's bag, or *anyone*'s pockets! I may be the only person in Honoria who has ever gotten away with going through a Monk's bag. One of my goofier-than-usual attempts at entertaining everyone had me acting like a hungry, drunken bear cub that thought Bet might have more wine in his bag. Bet laughed at his deranged adopted brother's behavior and no harm was done that day, but I strongly advise against doing anything like this as a rule.

"*Bai nai*" translates to "Where are you going?" It's the Honorian way of saying "What's up?" or "How are you doing?" It is just making small talk and not considered nosey. The locals are (almost) never intending to follow you to where you are going when they ask this question. If you feel uncomfortable about giving up too much information, just answer "hello" or "going home," and smile. It's better to be thought a friendly person who doesn't understand than to be thought unsociable.

Enjoy the national happiness, but stay awake and aware.

For the most part Honoria is a country of people who are kind and hospitable.

64

Freddy Farang

Fred is a decent and sociable German national. I like him. Most folks do. He just came back to Honoria. While here last year he met many of the same people who have since become my friends. They are his friends too. Fred came to the Temple this year. He wants to study meditation. He wants to open a meditation school in Germany when he returns there. Fred has no previous meditation experience. He will start from the beginning and is unsure if he will stay at the Temple for a few days, or perhaps one full week.

Fred met my ex-wife when he was here last year. I get the feeling he did more than just meet her. He asked me what went wrong. I told him very briefly about her contributions to the problem—the cold heart, bizarrely dysfunctional family history, and so on. I also told Fred about the problems with cultural adaptation she and I shared, and a few of the ways in which I had contributed to the problems. The explanation took no more than five or ten minutes. At the end of those few minutes, Fred said, in a lone word, that he was "surprised."

I was not surprised that Fred was surprised. Most people that knew my ex thought she was hotheaded and a bit hardhearted, but often likable. She was always pleasant with her customers.

Fred then expanded his reaction a bit by saying, "I just thought she was a good businesswoman." That was the end of our conversation.

Fred seemed to imply that being good at business could bridge the gap between emotional illness and marital bliss. But then again, Fred is going to open a meditation business with a partial week's experience for credentials. Few people truly become masters of meditation without many years of effort. No one in history has ever mastered meditation well enough to teach it in a single week.

Fred didn't either.

A very big mistake was made when I married my ex-wife.
She should have married Fred.

Fred's business oriented life and attitude have brought me to a deeper understanding of why the Honorians and so many other cultures would prefer we Westerners just visit, spend some money, and go home within a few weeks. There is something about us they can't trust. I understand that. There are some things about us that I don't trust.

I've been at the Temple for three months and am now accepted by the community to a much greater extent than I ever thought possible. The Monks and Nuns, of course, extend themselves to everyone—but now people of the village and even some people in surrounding towns have come to know and care about me. Some have even shown love and concern.

According to Arjan, Sepp, and a few others, the locals have seen enough generic decency in me to enable them to like me. They have seen "the alien" work hard to adapt, and to bring out the best in himself. I have also, at times, helped some of them to bring out a better part of themselves.

I don't have to hitchhike by sticking a thumb out or waving at drivers anymore. The little motorbikes (there are almost no cars) just pull over next to me when they see me walking down the road. They give me a ride to wherever I'm going.

I will still always be a farang. No matter what heartache I have shown them over lost love, the natives like to believe that their women are only sex objects to me. It must be easier than admitting that women are only sex objects to them.

No matter how many times they see me smoking hand-me-down leftover tobacco rolled in newspaper or calendar shards, they believe I have money somewhere. Lots of it. And just don't want to spend it. On anything.

It makes sense that these folks are skeptical of people from colonizing countries. Like a stepbrother who moved out of the house as a child and is only around on holidays, I will always and never be a part of the Honorian family. Even marrying their daughters and fostering their grandchildren would still leave me a step removed, as it has with so many of the expatriates I have spoken with about it. Equality is only granted in percentages.

These people believe that their reception would be no different, no warmer, no more inclusive, no better and perhaps a whole lot worse if *they* were suddenly dropped into a foreign Western country and culture. They are, of course, correct. My opinion of Honorians softens as I think of some of the crap given to foreigners in my own country.

65

The Warm-up

Arjan has just returned from a short road trip accompanied by a couple of Honorian spiritual heavyweights.

He and two senior Master Chanters from other monasteries have begun extended chants and instruction with the residents here. The Temple brothers and sisters are still smiling but there is also a more serious, studious look about them. It feels like the seniors are drill instructors readying troops for a formal parade in front of dignitaries.

The increased activity adds potency to everything the Monks and Nuns do. Even a foreign layman like myself can feel the intensity in the atmosphere. It is like a runner's high. I'm not an experienced "runner" in either the literal track and field sport or the metaphorical psychic track that these robed folks run on. The upgrade in atmosphere is making me a little bit dizzy, but luckily there seems to be some mysterious stabilizing agent helping me stay comfortable. It is probably the good influence and secure demeanor of my neighbors. The Monks and Nuns do seem more intense right now, but they are not acting nervous or overwrought. Whatever it is that they have been asked to do, they seem to have nothing but total confidence in the success of the operation.

I feel the same comfortable confidence and have to guess that being around them is starting to affect me in ways that might be similar to how the Monks and Nuns themselves are affected by the influence of their Buddha.

Like a runner's high, life seems to be on automatic pilot. I am gratefully "in the flow" that has been so often described by runners and LSD trippers. There is a continuous burst of celluloid clarity and effortless energy that seems to both originate from and arrive at the same special place of mental stillness and calm. It is the place all action comes from—the *being* from which all the doing gets done. That may sound strange, but practiced runners can tell you it is true.

The three Senior Monks seem to be showing their juniors how to build a vibe.

Although I don't know what is happening, a few things seem obvious. The first is that something powerful and positive is going on. The second is that I'm way behind everyone else here in knowing what that something is. The third is that if I knew what that something was, I likely wouldn't know what to do with it anyway. The fourth is that there's no possibility I'll be able to pay attention to anything else while this mental lightning is flashing.

There is more than just my usual language-and-cultural ignorance at work here. If my best friend were trying to explain it in perfect English, I still wouldn't understand. It is a for-real beyond wordser, but here are a few impressions.

Laughing at nothing, smiling at everything, concern for everything, concern for the molecules that make up everything, and concern for whatever makes up those molecules. This concern is not worried, but comfortable. It is a concern that is confidence-and-solution based without attachment to parent dramas or problems. Truth is so fantastic that fantasy is jealous. Lies are not possible. Simplicity is ornate. We are having the kind of fun that a child playing with twigs and pebbles could understand but no "sane" adult would.

I can't bother anyone here to attempt a long explanation in sign language right now. The icing on the go-teach-yourself cake is that everyone else is absorbed in his or her own intense process. The other residents may be more used to the high life than I am, but this elevation of focused energy and psychic connection is a cut above their daily levels too. They are busy with their own adaptations. To the extent that it can be true in a Temple full of Monks and Nuns, I am flying solo.

Some brain-flickerings from the power surge are more noticeable than others. Last night I actually wobbled out of the Temple from the intensity of the chanting. It felt like smoking a fat doobie of Da Kine would, but no herb was involved.

Aha! I just found out that there is going to be a festival at the Temple. That's what everyone is charging up for. It is time for me to stop everything else, relax, and work on balancing the elevated wavelength in time for the festival. There are seven days to sort this out before crowds from all over the province start filing in.

I won't be able to write any more this week.

66

The Festival

The warm-up week is now complete! Everyone is elevated and centered. I am more grounded and stable.

Being in the right place at the right time to experience a mass elevation of consciousness by Wisdom Professionals was not in my plans! Even the finest surprises, greatest events, and luckiest of breaks require that a person adjust to them. Luckily, humans can adapt well and grow from experience. I was too dizzy to find my feet when this started but am now much better prepared for dealing with the carnival trappings that have just arrived and the public that will arrive soon.

We are preparing for an unusual New Year's celebration. Three days of festivities will run Friday through Sunday. There seem to be several types of New Year happening at once. Secular and religious celebrations are on the schedule. This is a major occasion and has a much heavier spiritual side than our standard Western style New Year's Eve parties would.

It's early Friday morning and we are all doing the physical setup for the event. It is not just about putting a few tables here and a few chairs there. The Temple has taken on a carnival atmosphere that would make P.T. Barnum proud. Massive speakers pound out deafening music that rattles the cabins as far away as the mountaintop. Multicolored lights and flags are everywhere. The Monks and Nuns never lose their dignity, but it is obvious that they are having even more fun than usual.

The feeling on the Temple grounds is a combination of Heaven and open mike night at a trailer park that is well stocked with stimulants. The volume is several times louder than what you would hear in front row Metallica concert seats. Everyone is happy, but all the action seems a little schizophrenic compared to our usual serenity. Everyone's running around getting things *done*. The Temple is usually a place where the main focus is on *being* rather than doing (except for Arjan, who is always doing).

Arjan is rapidly becoming one of my heroes besides already being a teacher and benefactor. His selflessness is baffling. He doesn't seem to need any sleep. Three visiting Monks are in my usual cabin. A French visitor and I are sleeping in Arjan's cabin, at his insistence. Arjan himself is sleeping outside—if at all. He is nonetheless coordinating the whole show smoothly, calmly, and happily.

There are food tables, lights, and stages everywhere. Temporary buildings have been constructed in a single day with an efficiency that would impress the U.S. Army Corps of Engineers. Everything is coordinated to a much greater degree than it is ever discussed.

By five p.m. the preparation is complete. They tell me this first night will be lightly trafficked, but the place is done up as if the whole province will be here. The whole province may need hearing aids by festival's end. The volume of the multiple sound systems is deafening!

Stairway to the Goddess

(SATURDAY) THE BIG DAY
HAPPY NEW YEAR

Last night was loud, but very few people got a chance to hear it. Turns out that the day before the big holiday is a stay-at-home-and-pray-for-the-ancestors day. Most folks did.

But today everything started getting busy very early in the morning.

Blessings are being given throughout the grounds. The main station is about halfway up the hill toward the cabins, at the altar of the Female Deity of Compassion. Monk (formerly Mr.) Mee, Monk Chaiyote (The Living Yahk), Monk Tah Mak Wat Lo (the Senior Monk), and a few visiting Monks are giving Water Blessings up there.

The Water Blessing is a ceremony where a brush made of sticks is dipped into a bowl of consecrated water and then shaken over the heads of the faithful by Monks reciting prayers. Any water would be a blessing in this heat, but even devout cynics have reported "feeling something happen" as a result of this baptismal type of blessing. This water was given ritual attention for a long time by several powerful people.

There are enough firecrackers to rival a Fourth of July party at Coney Island. People light them by the hundreds in hopes of scaring away the evil spirits. These "evil spirits" are symbolic of personal bugaboos in the meditative sense, but they are also very real physical demons to those who perceive and believe so.

The altar closest to all this activity houses a statue symbolizing the female deity of compassion. People glue very thin, small, gold colored squares of foil on to her in respect. This statue symbolizes the virtues of compassion and is beautiful on any day. Covered in gold, she glows with the air of a Goddess on her wedding day.

The most amazing part of all this activity is the circulation of positive energy. It is very similar to what happens during our Morning Walk through the village, but even more intense at Festival time. The Monks bless everything and everyone. Everyone and everything blesses them back through thought and gratitude (as well as donations). This loop of good intent gathers strength through its continuity. The energy grows with each bit of well-wishing that the participants install. The exchange of respect, generosity, good wishes, and spiritual love becomes very intense. The whole becomes more than just the sum of its parts.

Firsthand experience of this phenomenon is not confined to Monks and Nuns. I've heard Westerners and Asians, cynics, believers and nonbelievers alike speak of "feeling the energy multiply." The exponential growth of this feedback loop of good will is, in fact, too obvious to ignore.

The fact that it is easily felt does not mean that the mechanics of this powerful force are easily explained. I know very little about it. What I do know is that the *Buddha Nature* is involved. The Buddha Nature is easily translatable into our culture and language as the Christ Spirit. (It also translates well into the languages of physics, psychology, philosophy, etc.) There are plenty of differences between Eastern and Western thought. This is not one of them. Christ Spirit and Buddha Nature both refer to the force that makes Mother Teresa, Gandhi, and Martin Luther King Jr. so very much more similar than the cultures they came from.

The Nuns and Monks are Buddha's (or the Enlightened State of Mind's) recognized representatives to the people, but each layperson also has the "Buddha seed" within. By virtue of simply being a human, pointing oneself in the right direction, and doing the necessary work, Buddhahood (Awakened Mind, Enlightenment, Salvation) can be attained.

The Goddess representing compassion

So the Monks and Nuns are not considered superhuman. They are recognized and respected by the villagers as regular humans who are very admirably exercising their most noble options in life on behalf of the village and the world. But due to this common belief that *every* human has the potential to become enlightened, there is equanimity with as well as a reverence for the clergy. This makes relations with the Monks and Nuns very familial and comfortable for laypeople, perhaps to a much greater degree than ours can be in the West.

I wish you were here. If you have enjoyed this book so far, you would love this party. Come soon. The Westernization and commercialization of this culture has already begun. There may be only a generation or two remaining where this lifestyle and these celebrations maintain their authenticity and power.

Knowing this makes the Honorian introversion and resistance to so-called progress seem more rational.

The prayer chanting session at noon is very powerful due to the week's intensive practice of our own residents and the addition of many visiting Monks. The chanting and its spiritual repercussions are what everything here is really all about. Everything else stops when it happens. It resonates through every cup of tea, plate of food, and bottle of ass-kicking rice wine. All things vibrate in tune with it.

The dogs don't even bark when it's going on. Well, most of them don't. There is one who sings along very well. There may be more to this peculiarity than meets the eye. I can't really say any more about it. (But the dog *does* have a fur structure that resembles a shaved head and a robe!)

Evening has arrived and the first actual drunk has arrived along with it. This guy has a two a.m. buzz at six p.m. In the man's defense he seems pleasant enough, it is a Saturday and a New Year's bash, and he has found a way for his mind to cope with the dizzying walls of noise coming from the multiple speaker systems. (The presenters of the various events seem to think sheer volume is the way to compete for attention.) It seems doubtful that our friendly buzzboy will be the last person we see under the influence tonight. With any luck, the respect everyone usually has for this place won't decrease as the alcohol consumption increases. The feeling I get from Mr. Plastered is that he and anyone in a similar condition will stay merry and peaceful.

It's eight p.m. now. I've been selling flowers and incense for the past few hours at the base of the stairway. People take these up the stairs as an offering to the female deity before they get their Water Blessing from the Monks. The Monks are still up there and have been since early morning. A sizable crowd has arrived by now. Honorians from throughout the province and beyond are here, and they seem to get a real kick out of watching a foreigner working for the Temple. I have become an attraction! They love watching me try to figure out how many flowers they want and what is the right amount of money to take. Everyone is very sweet and helpful to me—for two reasons. The main reason is that they are kind-hearted, helpful, small-town people. The other is that it *creates merit* for them to be so.

Extending kindness, especially in a Temple related situation, earns one a degree of personal positive energy. It is the same reason behind why, for the layperson's sake, a Monk isn't supposed to refuse anything offered to him by a layperson. As a representative disciple of the Buddha Nature, the Monk signifies an opportunity for the layperson giving that gift. It gives that layperson the opportunity to experience personal growth through selfless altruism to the Universe at large (as represented by the Buddha Nature that is represented by the Monk), thereby improving the giver's karma.

Of course, it works best when the giving is a heartfelt generosity and not done with a buying-off-God kind of attitude. It certainly feels like that right sort of generosity is going on here tonight.

It is ten p.m. and the party be jammin'! This spiritual carnival has turned into a magical experience. A karaoke stage and full drive-in-movie sized cinema screen are among the modern attractions. The more traditional activities are all hypnotically beautiful. They include an unusual stick shadow-puppet show with, of course, plenty of sound. The puppets-on-sticks are behind a screen with a light shining through it from behind the puppets, so the whole production is done as shadows.

My favorite stage is full of children doing traditional dancing. They are decked out in brightly colored birdlike costumes complete with headdress, a stand-up tail, and eight inch curved metal fingernails. The motion is poetic. The bodies move gracefully but most of the action is in the hand movements. The hands alone conjure up images of an underwater ballet. It is an extremely fluid production and *sooaye mahk* (very beautiful).

Eleven p.m. and the party remains both big and peaceful. Much to my surprise, the six p.m. drunk turned out to be the only one. He has actually become less wobbly by now and is helping with some preliminary clean up and maintenance.

I know a lot of the people here. It feels very warm and friendly. Many of the folks here have given me rides on their motorbikes or are people I silently visit every day on the Morning Walk. The village feels a lot like home now.

A policeman walks up to me and says hello. The uniform and gun don't seem to fit the kind-hearted person I know from Morning Walk. It takes a moment to recognize him as the person I have seen so often wearing plain clothes at his home in the village. He is one of the people who have been feeding me for the past few months.

I've either gone half deaf or adapted. The pain provoking walls of sound from the multiple speaker systems have toned down enough for me to be able to trace singular songs and speeches to their individual venues. Everything seems to be at a more reasonable level and easier to deal with.

It's not just me. All the Nuns and Monks who looked a bit tired and noise-addled earlier are recovered and pumped up. The energy continues to circulate and grow. Everyone is having fun. It is as comfortable a big party as I've ever attended.

After midnight the crowd starts to thin a bit but as with any big party, the music and dancing go on well into the wee morning hours.

SUNDAY

The walls of sound weren't turned off until three a.m. and were turned back on at seven. Staying in bed was pointless. It took just a minute of being pissed off to figure out that it was a better idea to stay happy. Getting irritated by the morning's lack of logic wouldn't accomplish anything.

Why is the sound cranked up to full volume for the benefit of the people who own the equipment? There's no one else here this early except the Monks and Nuns. They'd already had enough noise as of yesterday!

Mai mee pen ha! (No problem!)

Sepp always says, "Don't think."

166

"We should take care
not to make the intellect our god;
it has, of course, powerful muscles,
but no personality."

Albert Einstein

Sepp's and Mr. Einstein's ideas make a lot of sense this morning. It seems important to not think about anything that is out of my personal control and could lead to me being pointlessly pissed off and annoying. It seems a good time to turn the swirling brain off.

Right now I'm going to have a nice, big cup of shut-the-fuck-up and go be cheery for the benefit of the really tired people who have done most of the work. I'll go give the people in robes some amusement and lighten up their morning. Lordee knows they've done enough of that for me. I'll go do my clown dance for them before the crowds start filing back in.

We had some tired fun in the morning. It is now one p.m. and the crowds and noise are in full swing again. The Monks and Nuns will continue to gather energy. They will be pumped up for another round of major festivities this evening, but this alien's ears are ringing. I've been cheerful for as long as I can be cheerful. The Frenchman who had been sharing Arjan's cabin with me has already gone. If I go as well, Arjan may take his cabin back. He's been too kind already. He should have the option to rest in his own room if he eventually wants to do so.

I'm off to the beach in Bankrut town.

67

Mr. Noi and the Baanklangaow Resort/
Corporate Relations

Sepp has gone back to Germany for a little while. As soon as he left, the reception at the resort he managed got a lot colder toward our regular crew. The owners wanted a new image and the higher income they hoped it would bring. The smiling hospitality disappeared. It was replaced by some new tile on the patio and "When are you leaving" looks. A cloud of gentrification fell upon our watering hole. Maybe it will get better when Sepp returns, but for the time being the Baan Rim Haad Resort era is history.

No problem. I'm from New York City. I've seen this before. Owners figure they can get more money for the same product if they dress it up for sale to wealthier people. They buy up rental properties cheaply in low income areas, set rents to price the residents out of their homes, and install a few modern conveniences. Housing and services then become available only to the financially fortunate. This practice is partially responsible for the many displaced people who are wandering America's urban streets. They stare dumbfounded into windows of expensively remodeled housing units and fifty dollar a plate trendy restaurants that used to be their rent-controlled apartment buildings and corner stores.

Like only the luckiest former residents of those gentrified urban ex-neighborhoods, I found someplace else to go.

On days out from the Temple, I now go to see my friend Mr. Noi. He is the manager at the Baanklangaow Resort and something of a local business celebrity.

Before going to the Temple, I taught English to Noi and his staff for a month or two. The job paid less than survival rate but required only two hours a day of teaching time. It included meals and a single bed.

The mutual respect between the staff and myself has grown since I was their English teacher. It has improved to the point where I'm comfortable and at home here. Mr. Noi has invited me to forget the English lessons and just come to visit, eat at the breakfast buffet, swim in the pools or ocean, sleep in the guesthouse facility, and relax. No money down. I continue to be a very lucky man for more than material reasons. I have another good friend.

Mr. Noi buys me a few drinks now and then, but I turn down many of his offers. I've slowed the alcohol down considerably. We are both pleasantly shocked at the difference in my condition between when I first arrived at his resort and now.

I can't afford to drink at will now. This lack of alcohol funds would have bothered me into a seizure months ago. It is no longer a problem. Arjan's method of letting me stay in or go out of the Temple as I please is working successfully. "Let the job do itself," someone once said. I am absorbing more and more of Temple mentality by ordinary contact and some weird kind of psychological osmosis.

Arjan knows that a person needs to be treated as the person he is. He is smart enough to figure that a forced-march method of education will not work on a habitually independent fifty year old who grew up in the streets of Brooklyn, New York. Arjan feels that a life is worth saving, even if the rules need to be bent a bit to accomplish that. His actions and my reactions have confirmed all his theories and his hopes for me.

In spite of the obvious results, Arjan's methods are still looked upon as avant-garde. He is considered a very radical and controversial Head Monk by some local traditionalists.

Many others would be happy to defend him with their lives.

Let me tell you a little more about the beautiful combination of form and function that is Mr. Noi's place. Baanklangaow is often frequented by well heeled folks from the capitol city who are on holidays, vacations, and weekends, as well as by international tourists. The rooms here are almost always full. There is a highly acclaimed professional scuba school on the premises run by a Scandinavian husband and wife team. They speak five languages between them, are fun to drink with, and they attract people from all over the world.

By Honorian standards, BKA is an expensive resort. By American standards it is an expensive resort for Honoria, but at a price equal to that of a discount motel in the rural U.S. Anywhere in the world this place would be considered *high end*. High end just costs less here.

As in many fancy hotels, the staff is mostly composed of beautiful, smiling young women. They are not wearing the forced smile you see in many places around the world. These folks are genuinely happy to be here. They work long and hard, but get treated well and appreciate it. This satisfaction becomes contagious to the guests.

The resort was vacant acreage when its owner showed incredible faith in the inexperienced Mr. Noi. He gave Noi the money and responsibility to make this resort the fanciest place on Bankrut Beach. There are now two swimming pools, kayaks, ping pong, a computer room, room service, and much more available here. The vegetables served in the dining areas are organically grown on site. There is a master green-thumbed witch (in only the best sense of the word) running the organic garden's operation. This resort is one of only three to date that have won the Honorian government's highest ecological award. Mr. Noi put a lot of heart and thought into making this place a high class establishment without a pretentious atmosphere.

Miss Sohm at the front desk and Miss Jeab the bartender are extremely courteous and friendly. They are also beautifully sexy enough to be Playboy models. They're too genuine to fake a pose and too innocent to put themselves on display, but they do have the physical talent for the job. I've tried imagining it, as it would surely be a breathtaking view. It doesn't work. They've got a different and more innocent kind of sweetness. My attempts to picture them otherwise always end in the sick feeling a man might get if he suddenly realized that the woman lying naked on the bearskin rug in his daydream had his daughter's face.

Mr. Phuenk is the main driver for the resort and a companion/ go-for person to Mr. Noi and Noi's father. He is also the early morning supply house runner and the night auditor. He is strong, solid, loyal, and probably the most military person I've ever seen out of uniform. One gets the feeling that anyone posing a threat to this place could easily be delivered to the swamps by Mr. Phuenk. He brings to a Brooklyn mind the combined images of a Mafia soldier's loyalty and a Consigliore's (advisor's) intelligence. I'd want Mr. Phuenk next to me in any combat situation. I'm glad he is my friend.

As I've already told you, the sex-trade scene here makes it pretty easy to "get a twenty year old piece of fluff to help you burn off calories at less expense than a health club membership." I leave the phrasing just the way the pig-looking fellow at the bar here said it to me. There are a number of Westerners who come to Honoria just for the sex tourism. Miss Jing is the head of housekeeping. She is forty years old and skinny as a toothpick, but if I had knowledge of her language and anything to bring to a relationship with a woman, there would be no fluff hunting. I would bring my anything to Jing. She glows.

Sobha runs the kitchen and waitstaff. She is the captain of her ship. If the whole staff lined up together, you'd easily pick out Sobha as the person in charge. She is pregnant with twins. Although she's been carrying two babies for six months in eighty to a hundred-and-ten degree heat and high humidity, Sobha is often on the job from six thirty a.m. until nine p.m. She does physical as well as organizational work but somehow manages to stay both pleasant and efficient. There are few humans of any gender in any nation whose work ethic, stamina, and efficiency can compare with Sobha's.

Mr. Noi has recently made a clever adjustment in the ratio of wealthy to more down-to-earth clientele by adding a much cheaper guesthouse/hostel facility. The new socio-economic mix of clientele seems to have relaxed both staff and guests. It has also made for some pleasant and cooperative evenings around the bar. The folks with expensive luggage, especially the Honorian wealthy, don't want to look arrogant in front of the foreign backpackers. The backpackers don't want to look too "low rent" in front of the natives. A good deal of stress is taken off the staff while these groups educate each other.

CORPORATE RELATIONS

Everyone is nice to everyone here. They are all a little nicer to me. The staff and I get along well now, but it took some work to establish those friendships. I was suffering severe mental disarray and alcoholism upon arrival as their English teacher. I had moved into a very small room on the property with two duffle bags, my own large refrigerator full of beer, a cardboard box full of whiskey, a death wish, and not much else.

The rural staff members already had some misgivings about white folks in general before I arrived. Before the hostel section opened, they regularly dealt with fifty relatively rich and often demanding tourists for every single sociable one. (Many were Honorian nationals. Some were French, German, Scandinavian, or Aussie, with a few Americans in the mix.) The staff had no reason to think I would be more of a fellow employee than a pain in the ass.

I was nuts and they weren't aware that my inconsistencies were harmless. It is very understandable. Teachers are considered an extension of parents here. Honorian school teachers are highly respected role models, always formally dressed and sober in class. I must have looked like Godzilla to them. The crew averaged about five foot two inches tall and maybe a hundred and twenty pounds soaking wet with rocks in their pockets. How could a white alien over six feet tall and weighing two hundred pounds who is both drunk in the morning and yet a good teacher even exist, much less end up being as pleasant and harmless as a mango! It took them a while to understand that they were allowed to smile back at me.

Progress has been made on both sides. There is now an understanding and camaraderie between us. We are veterans who have graduated from ignorance. We are now able to understand each other much better—both as individuals and as products of our cultures. These days we nod, wink, and smile at each other a lot.

A nod, wink, or smile can mean more in some circumstances than it does in others.

Mr. Noi

Jeab and Sohm

Pregnant with twins, Sobha runs the kitchen

The Garden Wizards

Ms. Jing

Mr. Pheunk

68

Sunny's Place

Right down the road from Baanklangaow is Sunny's place. Sunny's is always packed with customers. On nights when other restaurants are so empty that closing wouldn't change the profit totals much, Sunny is keeping busy. The beer is reasonably priced, the food is great, and the ocean laps your toes at high tide—but that's not why the place is always full. It's Sunny. His name may actually be spelled Soni, or Sonny, or Sohni, but regardless, sunny describes his disposition.

As is true of many smaller local places, the staff here consists of a husband and wife, two daughters, and a sister. It's not just a business operation to these people. Family pride and unity insist on running the establishment well. How they run it tells you something about what "family" really means within the Honorian culture.

Everyone on the staff likes and loves each other. The boss/father is benevolent to all as well as firm in his conviction to run the best operation possible. It shows up in the quality of the food and service, and then in the number of people who return frequently.

For me the best part of Sunny's isn't what he sells, it's in *the hang*. I like to show up during slow business hours when few other folks are around. I go to hang out with the "Sun man" and crew, just to talk or watch TV with them.

Sunny is one of the only people in this area who is nearly fluent in English. He is a very social person who likes to practice and improve his English. Our conversations usually continue right through any TV program or business distraction.

One sociable human being who can speak English is about as valuable as oxygen around here. During the half of every year that foreign tourists disappear, conversation is a rare treasure. The nonverbal communication at the Temple is enlightening, but it takes a lot of work from someone who is as much of an amateur at it as I am. Sunny and you are the only folks I can talk with now that Sepp is gone.

Sunny would be a welcome friend in any community at any time of year. I always take my infrequent visitors to Sunny's first (after we've seen the Temple). If you ever spend an evening there, you'll understand why.

Sunny's Place

Sunny

69

Sunday in Bankrut

Street scene in Bankrut

At the beach, Bankrut

All ages enjoy their time together

Friendly drunken tourists

70

If It Doesn't Help, Don't Do It

I returned to the Temple after a few days of visiting Mr. Noi and Sunny. The three visiting Monks were still in my usual cabin. They are wonderful people. It is great to see them again. On the other side of the coin, after the festival and then a few days of Mr. Noi buying drinks for me, it would be nice to stabilize in familiar surroundings and quiet settings.

Not happening.

No problem.

I slept in the Temple itself that first night back and was looking forward to the Morning Walk. Two loud bongs on the Temple bell woke me before my travel alarm could go off. They were followed by a loud shriek from behind that shook me as I was rolling up my bedding. "Ten! Phra Bai Lao!" ("Ten! The Monks are already leaving!")

When Kumnung shrieked my name from behind, I ignored it. My first thought was to yell, "Please shut the fuck up!" at her. I quickly remembered that the morning after drinking vacation-quantities of alcohol is not the time to trust your first thought. I also remembered, "If it doesn't help, don't do it!"

My second and more subdued thought was, "This is not a good way to start the first morning back here."

Kumnung walked up to me and gave me the same information she had yelled before, but in a calmer and more hangover-friendly tone of voice. I thanked her. We both smiled and went about our business.

"If it doesn't help, don't do it!" is one of my old friend Andy's beautifully simple but brilliant lines.

I may have felt like snapping my sister's head off, but it would have accomplished nothing. It would have offended her, worked contrary to family relations, and had me feeling like a jackass within minutes.

"If it doesn't help, don't do it!" Anything else is self-sabotage. A lot of trouble has found my dumb ass because I forgot this simple rule. It's not good to hurt anyone's feelings (especially not your sister's feelings), but the person one always hurts the most when one does things that don't help is oneself.

You don't want to make your best friend feel like a jackass, and whether you are with a thousand compadres in a big city or live alone in a cave—*you are your own best friend.*

71

School Days

I am looking in all the area schools for work as an English teacher. Hanging out with kids is fun, and teaching English is the only work legally available to foreigners.

So far, I have only found one hour a week of teaching time. It's a very high paying position at two hundred Baht (US$4.80) for the hour. Of course, if you figure in the three hours travel time to the school and back, and the hundred and sixty Baht (US$3.84) it can cost for that taxi trip, it may take a while to put a down payment on that new Mercedes.

The kids and my Honorian teaching partner, Mrs. Yupa, make it all worth doing. It is also a chance to speak English with people who really want to speak it.

Honorians of all ages, but especially children, are very playful and love games of almost any type. If five minutes of teaching go by that are not fun, you've lost the class. A teacher trying to feed straight formula grammar to these children would be dead in the water as soon as he or she starts.

We sing a lot of songs and do a lot of make-believe store visits, mock telephone conversations, and the like. They love singing combined with motion. "If you're happy and you know it clap your hands"—clap, clap, clap.

The English language is the apparent reason I'm at the school, but as Mrs. Yupa has pointed out to me, it is really a secondary concern. At least as important is that the children feel comfortable speaking with foreigners.

Southeast Asian folks feel it is a *loss of face* to make a mistake and an even bigger loss of face to make a mistake in front of a foreigner. This applies to any aspect of life including the speaking of another language. If someone accidentally steps on your toe here they might say "Kor thot kahp" ("Excuse me"), but anything else in the way of an actual screw up pretty much gets treated as if the trespass were never committed. This is one of my pet peeves about the culture. Maybe the Honorian inability to apologize bothers me so much because of all the experience I've had apologizing. Very few people know as well as I do just how beneficial it can be to admit, "I'm sorry, I screwed up."

So I'm the guy who gives the children permission to use the erasers on their pencils. They are constantly hearing from me that "Humans always make mistakes," and "That's how we learn," and "It's no big deal," and "Good try! Thanks for playing!"

Wearing the white Temple suit to class helps. The children get an unconditionally trusted part of their culture mixed in with the unfamiliar American customs and language. Seeing the white suit relaxes them enough to soften the fear they have of my white skin, a foreign language, and making mistakes. It adds a degree of comfort to their learning experience. Any teacher of anything will tell you that a comfortable student is a better student. (Ask Arjan, if you don't believe that!)

Everyone needs a purpose—a cause or motivation that makes life a satisfying experience. Before my divorce, I had the motivation to help Honorian natives and all the tourists of various races and cultures to be more comfortable with each other. That motivation had a good plan attached to it.

The ex had a barely surviving, hole-in-the-wall pizza restaurant when I met her. I moved us into a bigger and much nicer building at a better location, and was in the process of opening a bar on the second floor when the divorce happened. It was going to be an officially anti-racist tavern. The place was widely publicized before it ever opened. Everyone in the area knew that this place, simply named *The Place,* was where racial barriers could be erased with alcohol. The first thing that went up was a sign in seven languages that read, "There are no Honorians or Farangs in here—only friends."

A hundred hours of my buying drinks for, and picking the brains of, the international population of Honoria had resulted in the menu in seven languages. To my knowledge it is still the only place in the world (and definitely in small town Honoria) with menus in Honorian, English, French, German, Italian, Spanish, and ET. The first page of the menu contained a box that said, "This menu is also available in Extra-Terrestrial language." It being a silent and psychic language, that notification probably wasn't necessary. (As you can see, the beer and weed here are strong enough to nourish an unusual sense of humor.)

Food could be shipped upstairs to the bar, drinks could be carried downstairs to the restaurant, both could also be enjoyed on the second floor outdoor terrace that overlooked the jungle, and everyone would live happily ever after.

Many a brilliant plan has been shot through the heart by one bad choice. I did not choose my partner wisely. I wanted this idea to work, found the wrong person to do it with, and married a *potential situation* instead of an actual woman. One day I sobered up enough to realize that we didn't belong in the same business or house together and that I'd rather relocate the dream than stay with the wrong person. Consistent intoxication has made idiots out of many otherwise intelligent people. I am one of them.

I learned my lesson—again.

So school days in their present form are not only a joy for the obvious reasons but also a bit of compensation for good efforts that have gone by the wayside.

Learning English may help these children break down some discomfort and prejudice. Maybe these fifty young children can erase more racial fears and emotional barriers in one hour a week than the drunks at my bar would have erased in a lifetime.

I continue to hope so—and to work on next week's lesson plan.

72

How to Get Your Prayers Answered

I feel a little uppity and out of place entitling a chapter "How to Get Your Prayers Answered." Everyone who has ever lived has asked this question at least once. It seems unlikely that a person like myself could find any important information about getting prayers answered while rooting through decades of deep intoxication and a few layers of insanity—and rarely saying a prayer or even believing in the concept.

It seems I may have gotten lucky.
There are three steps to getting your prayers answered. They are:

~ 1 ~

Set your hope, wish, prayer, aspiration, desired intent exactly where you want it, worded so that it is short, focused, and sticks to basics.

If your wish includes doing harm, or is of no benefit to others, restructure it. For a first step example, "I hope that nasty bastard dies painfully and that I never meet another asshole like him" probably won't work too well. "I hope to never meet nasty people from now on and that everyone else has the same good luck" is much better, but not quite good enough. The desired result needs to always be framed in positive achievement. The "I hope..." sentence should be structured to say something like, "I will meet nicer people and be one. I welcome all help with this."

To really want to make big points with the system, say something like the following *and mean it*. "I will meet nicer people and be one. I hope that all people, especially that one who has recently acted so nastily toward me, become decent and happy. I thank everything in existence (or God, any representative or representation of God, The Universe, The Force, The Collective Unconscious, Nature, Fate, Circumstance, Coincidence, Physics, or whatever name you have for your Bigger-Than-You thing) for help."

The language of positive direction and a benevolent intent are extremely important! Use them. The potent effect of positive language can be seen in Mother Teresa's comment, "I won't go to your anti-war rally. If you ever have a peace rally, call me."

~ 2 ~

Empty your mind of everything else.

Don't treat this step lightly! It is not as simple as it sounds. Most folks can't sit for a single minute without having a thought. Clearing mental clutter will take some work, but it can be very enjoyable. Relax through any initial bits of impatience.

Here's why this step is so important. Everything comes from nothing. Whatever you want to put anywhere starts with it not being there yet. Consider that nothing always comes before something. That's why it can truly be said that there is no thing as real as nothing.

Any background is the birthplace of whatever stands out from it.

Then consider that there can only be 100% of anything and so there can only be 100% of a mind. If 90% of it is rattling around on things other than those that we want in our line of focus, other than fulfilling the prayer-well, you can do the math. The percentage of random thought prattling around the brain needs to be reduced as thoroughly as possible in order to have most of the brain available to focus on getting intentions fulfilled.

Thoughts will pop up, but don't pay attention to them. Pay attention to the awareness that is recognizing them. To stabilize this ability will take patience, confidence, and consistent effort. There are tried and true methods that have been proven to work. My Temple mates and their ancestors have been using some of them for thousands of years. I strongly recommend a tried and true method because employing your own unassisted mind to clean out the clutter spawned by that very mind would be similar to hiring soldiers to end the concept of war. There are a lot of dead soldiers who would like to tell you that this logic is fatally flawed.

Finding a good teacher with whom a good working rapport can be established is extremely beneficial to your mind-clearing process. The quality of attention paid by a student is more important than who the teacher is—but just a bit. Finding a spiritually qualified, dedicated teacher *and* bringing all of yourself to the learning process are both very important.

Being overanxious can work against a person who is picking a coach, teacher, or guide. It's a wonderful thing to get help with this mind-clearing part of the prayer-fulfilling process. But just because one is well motivated and anxious to start doesn't mean that the first person to come along with a robe, a divinity degree, or a crystal ball is the right teacher. Try a few sessions each with as many teachers as you care to, and with an open mind. When the right time, person, and system for you arrive, it will be obvious.

> *"We should be very careful who we establish a relationship with as a teacher. First we should check him or her out and allow him or her to check us out. If this doesn't work out, don't push it. It is always better to develop a relationship that we can trust, rather than getting into one we are not sure of. This is essential advice. The student and the Lama have to have a strong faith and trust in each other."*

Lama Karma Rinchen

~ 3 ~

Take #1, plant it in #2, and don't ever give up.

Take the wish/dream/intention/hope/aspiration/mantra/prayer phrase from #1 and give the thinking of it as much attention as possible. Obviously, this should not be done while driving a car, crossing a busy street, working with a power tool, if baby needs immediate attention, or if the house is on fire. Keep your wits about you. Stay awake.

The aspiration, prayer, or whatever you want to call it will reach both its internal and external sources with the continuing practice of it, and you'll notice something else too. It will become fun to do this. You'll start making sure that the amount of time given to the process grows. The fun you are having and the fulfillment of your wishes will sprout and grow like everything does—from nothing into something, from a mere seed into a living, thriving entity.

The focus phrase/prayer can always be adjusted, amended, or altogether changed if it becomes appropriate to do so. As long as it contains the elements of doing no harm, benefitting more than just the self, a positive motivation and goal, and there is enough mental space for it to live and breed in, that prayer will inevitably be answered. How fast or completely it is answered depends on the practicality of the request, the honesty of altruistic intent, perseverance, strength of conviction and confidence in the process, stress-free determination, grace, patience, and of course the amount of time spent planting and watering the idea in our little and Big Brains. (Don't go schizo! They may seem like two separate brains sometimes, but there is only one of you.)

As the lottery people say, "You've got to be in it to win it." But the odds are a lot better of this process succeeding than are the odds of winning the lottery.

Available methods of emptying the mind and concentrating focus have been proven, century after century. A relaxed, consistent effort will pay dividends more valuable than money can buy. (These dividends can also include money, if the desire for it is based in well motivated goals and not selfish greed.) These dividends are guaranteed to increase as your diligence does. There aren't many lotteries with guarantees like that.

73

Buddhism's Big Kahuna

There are several interpretations of the term "buddha." It literally translates to English as "Awakened One," but the word can and has been used as an adjective as well as several variations of noun.

The historical Buddha that most folks refer to when they talk about Buddhism was an Indian prince named Gotama Siddhartha who lived about twenty five hundred years ago. Gotama led a sheltered and luxurious life in his father's palace until he sneaked out and saw the world's suffering. Deeply touched by a desire to help alleviate that suffering, Gotama sacrificed all his wealth, privilege, and earthly pleasures to look for the cosmic clue that would bring the height of his intuition to the forefront in every given situation. Gotama did this in order to become adept at giving meaningful assistance to any creature in need. He searched for Enlightenment and found it.

Buddhism can be thought of more as a scientific, psychological school of thought than what we in the Judeo/Christian/Muslim world would consider a religion. It contains no creator God, and it is common knowledge that the historical Buddha was a man, not a god.

One of the main things this man had to say was that we all have the Buddha Seed, *the potential to be enlightened*, within ourselves. Enlightenment and happiness are more a matter of cultivating that seed's growth than they are a matter of being born special. Anyone can bring great potential to life through sustaining good motives and constructive effort.

Most folks think the Buddha was born a little more special than the rest of us. The Buddha himself would probably disagree.

So, what we call Buddhism can be described as a school of thought based on a great man's observations and experiences, especially in the field of compassionate motivation.

A person of any religion can study the Buddhist school of thought, as it requires no trading-in of or conflict with other gods or cultures. There are Catholic and Protestant Buddhists, enough Quaker Buddhists to have spawned the term *Quakabu*, and enough Jewish Buddhists for the term *Jewbu* to have been invented.

The idea behind Buddhist practice is to consistently move toward becoming the best and happiest person one can be, in a way that also benefits others. An important part of that idea is to increase and stabilize tendencies within oneself that point toward the good stuff, and to make those tendencies a consistent director. Find your best stuff and exercise it until it gets strong. The system supposes that our individual responsibility is to experience, receive, and foster kindness as well as offer it to others. Everyone experiences varying degrees of success in cementing the good stuff to their character. The degree of success usually depends on how much attention is paid to the process.

Princely decency often shows up on folks who were not born princes. The late Mario Bruno lived in Brooklyn, New York and worked loading trucks with newspapers for forty years. He was all heart, strongly Catholic, and closer to being a buddha than many priests or any millionaires I've met.

I'm financially destitute and live alone in a bare cabin with a straw sleeping mat for furniture. I'm closer to *It* now than when there was a lot more luxury in my life. All the people around me have less stuff than I do. They're much closer to *It* than I am. This doesn't mean that Buddhists recommend destitution and poverty as a path to Enlightenment. They don't, and neither did the Buddha himself. The point is that having a lot and looking good do not necessarily translate into knowing good, much less doing, feeling, or being good.

Much of modern life is based on surface appearances rather than deeper reality. In Buddhism, the "beauty is only skin deep" and "talk is cheap" sentiments carry a lot of weight. Wanting to help lighten suffering wherever possible is the biggie. Wanting to attain buddhahood for the right reasons is more important than having a precise definition for the word "buddhahood."

Buddha may have actually invented the idea of feeling equal compassion for all suffering people, regardless of whether the people doing the suffering seem to deserve compassion or not. This notion is a lot more practical than it may appear at first glance. If we don't extend intelligent decency to the nastiest people, they won't know what intelligent decency is or how to eventually become a person who lives by it.

Being nice to the nasty may be wise, but living in this Temple has also shown me the other side of the coin. It helps to keep the company of those who have been traveling in the direction you want to move. You won't learn much about becoming an electrician from hanging out with prison guards or ballerinas. Student loggers won't get useful logging tips from lawyers or bakers. If you want to be at peace with the world, if you want to learn how to be a buddha, it helps to hang out with folks who are half way there themselves—whether they are Monks or Marios.

Even without any deep research or a teacher, as soon as you start to dabble in this stuff one thing becomes glaringly obvious. If you are motivated toward the kind of deeper goodness that requires a concern for others, everything that could be referred to as buddhahood or a quality of enlightenment has a better place to land on you (or more accurately, a better opportunity to surface from within you). The *concern for others* referred to above includes all living creatures, not just friends and family.

Anyone who wants to become a buddha has the Buddha's blessing—if they have their own.

"There is no ice or snow apart from water. The buddhahood of ordinary people can be likened to snow and ice melting and becoming water. From the beginning nothing has ever been lost."

Bassui

"Sentient beings are intrinsically Buddha...
like the relationship between water and ice."

Hakuin

The Awesome Nature of Southeast Asia

"A human being is a part of the whole called by us universe, a part limited in time and space. He experiences himself, his thoughts and feeling as something separated from the rest, a kind of optical delusion of his consciousness. This delusion is a kind of prison for us, restricting us to our personal desires and to affection for a few persons nearest to us. Our task must be to free ourselves from this prison by widening our circle of compassion to embrace all living creatures and the whole of nature in its beauty."

Albert Einstein

74

Nature

Honoria is one of the most beautiful countries on Earth. Breathtaking geological formations, diverse plant life, and exotic animals strike awe and awaken ecstasy in scientific researchers and starry-eyed tourists alike.

The natural world is rhythmic. It is more poetic than a blacktop and concrete world can imagine. It has soft shoulders and a more spatial logic than our linear daily patterns can imitate. Nature is woven of curves. It is connected to itself.

Regular prose can strain itself into cramps while attempting to describe nature. It pushes uphill bravely in places, but can't often get the job done.

Even poetry can fall short. Verbal drumbeats within a lyrical chorus help, but our culture holds itself apart from nature more often than it sees itself as part of nature. Suffering that attitude, there's only so close we can get to a partnership with or even a good description of the natural world.

Garden of Eden type metaphors were around long before the biblical version came to us. Gardens of Eden were too. At one time, people actually lived as integral parts of a world where every creature realized its dependence on and integration with nature. Nature enjoyed ultimate respect. Some folks, in some places, still have that kind of respect for it. Many others are busily moving back toward the reunion and cooperation with nature that may be the missing ingredient to insure our survival.

The Southeast Asian natural scene contains a million beautiful participants, but no part is as striking as the whole. *Nature,* as a unit, can repair any part of itself that needs help. The Honorian jungle, elephants, and ocean are legendary—but as you will see, a small Preying Mantis can provide the most awesome natural insight of all.

75

It'll Fix Itself

A famous Americanism says, "Nothing fixes itself." This is a sort of qualifying expression for the Yankee "Can do" or the Southern "Let's git 'er done." Other cultures think differently about this. Honoria is one of them.

In a culture that houses the belief in reincarnation among its primary tenants, nothing needs to be done very quickly. "Time heals all wounds," as they say, and within the framework of eternal rebirths there doesn't seem to be any shortage of time. Natural process is often allowed to amble along and take its course.

Sometimes this notion is taken to such an extent that it borders on the absurd. Sometimes it crosses the border. My friend left a motorbike with a broken engine in his yard for six months and waited for it to repair itself. Once a month or so he would actually go over to it and turn the key to see if the motor had fixed itself and was ready to hit the road again.

Living organisms are more adept at this "It'll fix itself" process than are manufactured things. In nature, "It'll fix itself" often works as accepted fact. I've seen it happen this year.

I have watched a slashed-and-burned field next to the Temple turn itself back into lush vegetation. No work, cultivation, or other human interference was involved. Nature just took its course.

I have also been such a field.

The restorative power of Nature is an effortless, bona fide miracle. Being in tune with Nature makes us a part of it and allows us access to its miraculous healing abilities.

A close relationship with Nature is a major part of the lives of these Buddhist Monks and Nuns that I live with.

76

Jungle

Nothing is greener
Drums beat from lizard throats
Steam as air rises everywhere
from self-recycling vegetation

Even the Natives don't go too far in
It would be easy (and could be fatal) to lose the way out
Birds' orchestral symphonies are freelance but tightly spun
Instrumental coordination of so many singing as one
yields enchanted melodic quality at precision intervals, with epic beauty

This original melody has inspired every music in human history
Harmonies are rhythmic ecstasy and functional communication
Wasted doing is replaced by functional being that gets everything done
Participants are individually free as ether, as all individual creations
disappear into the unified fabric of Jungle

Composed of an awesome and intimidating power that protects it,
The Unit commands greater respect than even its greatest creatures
Tigers, Elephants, and Cobras bow to it
Gods worship it

> Welcome to Earth
> as it *all* used to be
> Its billion creatures sharing a singular breath
> and a singular heartbeat

77

Sunrise

78

Rain

Flowers

80

Swamps

81

Sunsets

CHAHNG/Sacrifice

Chahng is the Honorian word for Elephant
Chahng is the heart and soul of the country's demeanor
Strength of Hercules, Character of Athena
As plow and tank, Chahng was the might of the kingdom
Supreme ruler of cultivated field, village, jungle, and battlefield
At once mighty and gentle
A true mother in every aspect
Provider and nurturing protector
Exemplar for mighty and benevolent kings

In its natural environment
Chahng is unconquerable
Who would want to conquer Chahng?
To love her is congruent with Nature!

Nothing ever has or ever will defeat Chahng—except us,
the people she has given her life for and with blind faith
entrusted her life to
We treat her with superficial respect
but have not thanked Chahng for her loyalty and service,
not even with the token gratitude of insuring her survival

We have not thanked Chahng for her
Sacrifice

Ocean

There's no need to go on and on with that "brilliant greens and blues" thing. You know what color the Ocean is. Millions of features and myriad creatures thrive past the beaches for incredible reaches below.

It gives life to everything and can take life from anything.
In no other place do so many things happen simultaneously.

In
No
Other
Place
Do
So
Many
Things
Happen
Individually

The word "Ocean" conjures up images so powerful that I would fear retribution for spelling it with a lower case "o."

Everyone, even if they live mid-continent, knows about The Ocean.
No one is unimpressed by its grandeur.
It has always been "the greatest show on Earth."

When it dies, so will we.

84

Survival

It's a dog eat dog world. It's all about killing things and eating them. Bugs eat plants, birds eat bugs, animals eat birds, and humans eat everything. Almost nothing that is eaten continues to live in its original form, so this whole process requires a lot of murder.

There are several ways in which spiritual peoples deal with this little Earthly quirk of fate. There's some great material from the Cherokee-based Good Medicine Society that describes "The Give Away." They say it beautifully. Their words on this subject strike a similar chord with those of a great many compassionate schools of thought.

Nothing living would exist without something else dying to support it. Be happy and gracious, grateful and humble about it all when you are eating— or when you are being eaten.

Joseph Campbell, one of our modern age's most beloved and brilliant teachers, said with a hearty laugh in reference to this business of killing and eating, "You take part in it!" This is the way it is. Be gleeful enough about living to take part in the system in as kindly a manner as possible, in spite of the system's apparent brutality. The Buddhists and many others often refer to this same attitude as "joyful participation in the sorrows of the world." This of course does not mean that we should rejoice when something sorrowful befalls us, but rather that we are here and have to deal with the situation as it is. The best option available is to be happy and forgiving—as well as speedy, strong, and clever!

The Monks and Nuns here are very good at managing this unavoidable contradiction of loving everything while killing and eating some of it. They treat life as very precious due to its fleeting nature (and delicious flavor). They take special pains to do no unnecessary harm to anything, and to show understanding when harm is done to them. They treat any unavoidable earthly harms with an acceptance of natural process and compassionate forgiveness.

Many Westerners are more confused about this situation than the Cherokee, Mr. Campbell, or the Monks and Nuns seem to be. I am one of those confused Westerners.

The blatant compassion/brutality schism of our earthly paradise/carnal hunting ground often makes life seem like a B-grade vampire-versus-zombie movie. Many of us counter with the attitude that whatever tries to stick its fangs in our neck is going to get a heart full of stake and a few bulbs of garlic stuck in the hole.

But whether we react with fear or compassion, there is no getting away from the bizarre fact that survival insists upon killing and eating some form of our neighbor.

Here in Honoria, they have the courage to call it like it is. In Western culture there is only one type of meat we call by the same name as the animal donating it. This animal has, strangely enough, become the symbol for a lack of courage. It is of course chicken. Maybe such a symbolic coward doesn't deserve a special name for its meat? Cow meat is beef and pig meat is called pork in our Western world.

Not so in Honoria. Cow and pig are the names of both the animals and the tasty, fleshy remains of those butchered creatures that so many of us humans feast on. Greater respect seems to be given to the meat than to the living creature it comes from. Humans...

I have to tell you the truth here. I don't know what the hell the point of this letter to you is. The subject bothers me, I don't know what I'm trying to say, and I don't much like the tone of the writing either.

(So I crumpled this page into a ball, threw it at the trash bag and missed. It landed on the floor. I left it there and lay down on my straw sleeping mat to invite more pleasant thoughts. Here's what happened.)

PRAYING MANTIS, PREYING MANTIS

Ever spend a couple hours watching a bug? I've been watching the Praying Mantis on my window screen for about two hours now. It is a hypnotically beautiful, musically graceful creature. It bobs up and down in a motion of poetic beauty that reinvents ballet. To humans, it looks like it is praying. To the unsuspecting spider whose life was just snuffed out by this Mantis, it probably looked like grass in the wind at first, then ferocious magic, and finally death. All Mr. Mantis ever saw was food.

Welcome to Earth. Make the best of it.

Reincarnation

Whatever has been reeling me in by the skin of my sanity has finally gotten through to me. Dues have been paid, lessons learned, death delayed, and karma burned. Past dramas had sponsored some dangerous traumas that will not return. A degree of immunity has been earned.

Redirected memory has changed my address mentally and brought me to a harmony where demons cannot find me again. It's the end, my friend, of a threatening bend in reality. Hell has, at least temporarily, given up the chase and allowed my own pace to flourish.

Life has become more of a friend to celebrate with than a threat to be defended against. Reincarnation has arrived with common sense as its vehicle and without any need to change bodies.

I hope that all your troubles lead to reincarnations.

Everything from complex world problems to tangled personal emotions appear different now than they did just a few months ago. A fresh life requires, learns, breeds, and is inspired by fresh points of view. The Wisdom Professionals here see everything from flowers, snakes, and locking doors to change, coincidence, and opinions in a much different light than we Westerners usually do. Their unspoken views have tempered mine.

85

Just a Coincidence

I just spent an hour trying to get the electric light to go on in the cabin. I fooled with it a bit but no go. Monk Bet lives right next door, down the hill about twenty yards or so. He is the house electrician here in both the physical and metaphysical senses.

It is too late in the evening to bother him now. We all did more physical work than usual today. He's probably resting and may even be sleeping. It seems best to just write myself a note. "Ask Bet to please look at the light tomorrow." OK, done.

I'll give the light switch that one last "goof flick" and go to sleep. Most folks will do the goof flick thing. You know what I mean. When something's broken and you've resigned yourself to the fact that it's not going to work, you give the switch one more flick just to show yourself that you've tried everything possible. Doing this makes the effort to get the thing working officially over and closes the case. I thought to myself, "No problem. Darkness is cool. Nice change of pace," as I gave the switch a goof flick. The light came on as if there was never a problem. It seemed to have fixed itself—or did it?

Monk Bet has never come to my cabin during the months I've lived here. Five minutes after the light came on, he knocked on my door. With a wide, sly smile he shrugged a communication that there was nothing special about his being there and said two of the dozen or so words that he can almost pronounce in English. "Chus visteg." ("Just visiting.") I invited him in. He had a light bulb with him.

With a wide, satisfied grin Bet looked up at my working light for longer than was sensible and then winked at me as if he was proud of himself. He lifted his right hand to show me the burnt out light bulb that he held in it. He shook it next to my ear so that I could hear the tinkle of its broken filament and then threw it in the trash bag.

How the hell did he change the light bulb before coming into the cabin? It seems he wasn't as tired as I had thought.
Most of you will say, "It's just a coincidence."
I agree.

But we don't all get the same meaning from that word, do we? "Co-incidence" may not always be the innocent bystander that we suppose it to be.

Bet decided that we should go uphill to visit Monk Mee. I thought it a bit late for visteg, but was glad to be asked along. We left the light on in my cabin. It glowed through the hole-in-the-wall window. I looked back at it in stunned amazement. All evidence suggested that Bet had somehow replaced that light bulb without being in the cabin.

Monk Mee was awake. He was trying to get a little radio I had loaned him to work.

It had a problem in the switch.

Bet fixed it.

As I once heard a Native American say, "Coincidence may just be the Great Spirit's wish to remain anonymous."

86

Buddha with the 7 Cobras

Of the hundred or so Buddha images in the Temple, my favorite shows the Buddha sitting with seven Cobras curving over his head in a protective canopy. There's a bit of space in between each Cobra, but that's no contradiction to the metaphor. Trouble couldn't even find its way into this Temple much less the space between the Cobras on that Buddha statue.

This bronze cast sculpture is visually striking. It nailed my attention at first glance. I began to focus on it, look into the history and legend behind it, and feel what it seemed to symbolize.

The snakes were awe-inspiring. In Eastern thought they represent the Great Temporal Protectors. The ability to shed their skins and grow new ones symbolizes the ability to throw off death and reincarnate within this field of time and space where we all physically live. It is also a metaphor for the abilities to adapt naturally and comfortably to drastic changes and new conditions. Day after day I sat focusing on these magnificent symbolic bodyguards of the Buddha, himself the symbolic embodiment of Enlightened, Awakened Thought.

You can only stare at something for so long before your mind starts to make things happen.

After sitting with the statue for several hours daily over a two week period, the Cobras appeared to start dancing. After watching a few minutes of Cobra dancing, I heard a whisper.

"I'm in here." It sounded like the whisper was actually happening physically, whispered into my ear by a friend three inches away—but I knew it wasn't.

"I'm in here," it repeated. My attention moved from the Cobras to the Buddha image itself.

"Let the snakes do what they do. You are supposed to be In Here. The snakes are there to prevent anything else from preventing you from being in here. Do not limit yourself by being in awe of the snakes. Pay attention to what you came here for!"

I still meditate often with the Buddha and Seven Cobras statue, but now—and with all due respect to my serpentine brothers—I redirect my attention a few inches to absorb the object of their protection.

Buddha with the 7 Cobras

87

Flower

This is a very well known story. You may have already heard something very similar to what's on this page. It is the most famous story ever told about the Buddha. Its lesson is also the central beam that supports the lives of the Monks and Nuns here, most Buddhists everywhere, several of quantum physics' greatest proponents, and the mystics of nearly every spiritual tradition that has ever existed.

In the Buddha's most famous teaching, he simply held up a flower and said nothing. One or two disciples out of a crowd full of wise folk and seekers got it. Here, in a Brooklyn accent, is what I think I may have learned from the Buddhists about The Flower.

The flower personifies all of Nature's wonder.

There is so much more to Nature and so much more to life than meets the eye. Not only is there more to Nature than meets the eye, but it may be that the birthplace of *all information* is in *anything* that exists or occurs naturally. Sounds weird? It did to me too.

There are two parts to this flower-says-it-all idea.

The first part would be the more obvious.

The flower doesn't exist.

Well, of course it does exist in everyday material reality. We can smell, see, and touch it. We can see the flower itself easily enough, but looking deeper we see what really makes up that flower. We can see how the flower is not a flower at all so much as it is a conglomerate, an aggregation of component parts. It has no essential or *intrinsic* (Latin root meaning *inward*) independent existence of its own. The flower tells the tale of how all things are interdependent and each thing is part of a much bigger picture. It lets us know that *nothing* really exists as a self-arisen, independent phenomenon.

The history of the soil that is composed of previously living materials including deceased flowers, the nutrients from the soil, water and every component molecule of hydrogen and oxygen that make up that water, the bacteria in the water—all these are essential parts and processes of our flower. The sun joins the plant in its photosynthetic process. Each of the many individual facets and functions of that food-producing operation are part of the flower. There is the color green itself, both composing and housed within the stem and leaves that support the flower. Then there is the involvement of insects in pollination, cross-pollination, and therefore evolution. There is the process of the flower's growth from seed through bud to flower. The flower is everything it has ever been as well as what it is.

Interdependent parts and functions all combine in mysterious, miraculous ways to become the flower. All of these parts are essential to the flower's existence. The flower is not the flower without the aggregates that compose it.

On a more esoteric plane, there's the romance and creativity that the flower sponsors in the human imagination—begging the famous question from the LSD era, "Is the human imagination awakened by the flower or does the flower itself come from the imagination?" The common answers to that question included "Who cares?" "Pass the joint!" "It is what it is," and "Everything is everything."

Above is the first part of "the flower" story.

The second part is the same as the first, only different. The difference would be shifting the first part's realizations from the little brain to The Big Brain. By increasing the percentage of mind being used, by broadening the focus and quality of attention being paid to this flower as an interdependent aggregation of component parts, the depth of our realizations are increased.

We can walk in the desert parched and pained, knowing that there is such a thing as water. The idea of finding it and the dream of its reward are comforting. The sight of an oasis, even if it is a mirage, brings hope. But actually tasting a refreshing coolness relieve your parched throat while every cell in your body rejuvenates with a vibrant hydroelectric power that regenerates life back to where you want your life to be is another thing altogether.

That is the difference between parts one and two, the little brain and The Big Brain understandings, of The Flower.

every thing is indeed Everything

Flower

88

A Week in the Cave

Impenetrable domain. Solid Rock. Solitude's fortress.

Thoughts and emotions have nowhere to go. Emptiness is their only company.

The first day is not as silent as you might think it would be. The invading noises of bats, jungle, and ocean blend in flurried motion to become that deeper internal silence that negates *all* commotion. Disturbing isolation becomes a comforting meditation.

Manufactured realities melt into amorphous ecstasies and play havoc in the shadows.

Isolation breeds clarity. Clarity breeds an intelligence that blends with memory to recall connections to people, places, things, emotions, events, everything. Soon memory fades as *Presence* takes over accompanied by knowledge with no fixed focal point. Neither concrete word nor abstract thought can say what this knowledge knows. Attempts to describe concepts so far beyond words bring a sense of irony that turns to laughter. That laughter may be as close as we can get to a definition of these mysterious concepts.

This type of knowledge, once accepted and embraced, leads to a tranquility of mind. The calmer mind uncovers an even more intensified depth of mental clarity. This intensified clarity welcomes a surprisingly potent peace. This peace announces that it is not a surprise. It has always been within and always will be. It never needs to arrive. It only needs to be recognized. And now, thanks to the magic of undistracted attention, it has.

This could happen in your bedroom or even your bathroom, couldn't it?

"We have been led astray through ignorance
to find a split in our own being...
there was from the very beginning
no need for the struggle between finite and the infinite...
the peace we were seeking has been there all the time."

D.T. Suzuki

89

Change

Many Buddhist folks refer to change in terms of "impermanence." I've seen Monks build a Sand Mandala. It is a very intricate and artistic sacred design that is carefully constructed by masterful hands from very thin lines of colored sand. It takes a long time to make. Great effort and devotion are spent for its sake. After weeks of perpetually prayerful effort, a precise masterpiece and meaningful icon has been created.

They let everyone look at this awesome accomplishment for a bit. Then they scoop up all the sand and pour it into the river. There's no attachment or regret. No "Oh! This one's too nice to let go. We should keep it." There is instead a chord struck in harmony with material reality. That's the way it goes. That's how the system works. Impermanence.

Change.

Change doesn't seem to know or care about beautiful, ugly, rich, poor, good, evil, what color an individual is, or what culture they come from. Change treats one-day mosquitoes, thousand-year redwood trees, and everything else equally.

Humans make judgments. Change is good or bad only according to who looks at it. The relativity of change is described very well in an old expression that says, "A beautiful woman is a joy to her lover, a distraction to a Monk, and lunch to a pack of wolves." Change is like that beautiful woman.

If everyone suddenly changed into people who *insisted* that governments smarten up, it would be a very bad thing for weapons manufacturers.

Other folks would look at it differently.

I have changed over the past several months. So have you. I may be in a position to notice my changes a bit more than most people. That's only because observing every thing, especially one's own mind, is such a big part of life at a Temple. We make a lot of time to observe changes here. I've even had time to write about them.

I'm grateful for having had the time to appreciate my changes, but in the future I'll find a better way to do it. There must be smarter ways of finding time to examine changes than to have a mental breakdown force the issue. Maybe keeping an eye on smaller changes earlier, more attentively, and more consistently from now on will help avoid some of the bigger, less pleasant, and more disastrous "holy shit" type changes.

Real changes, big changes, seem to happen slowly. Sometimes that fact is obvious, sometimes not. What looks like an overnight change has usually been building gradually for a very long time. A reporter once asked Bob Seeger how it felt to be an overnight success, selling millions of recordings. The reporter hadn't done his homework. He didn't know that Mr. Seeger had been grinding out a living as a local musician, playing small Detroit area bars for twenty years before his luck picked up.

Change can happen quickly too! I have things in my duffel bag left over from previous lifetimes. Sometimes we get stuck with old baggage. But that can also be changed.

Is there something you want to change about your life but think it can't be done? You should know that *Change*, itself, disagrees—and it is a lot more permanent and powerful than any problem.

"There is nothing in the universe that is a noun. Everything is a verb. A noun is a convention of language, not an expression of truth. There is nothing in the universe that stands still, even for a second. Any noun is a dynamic process, not a structure."

Deepak Chopra

90

Laughter

This psychological orgasm contains goodness too potent to control as joy, happiness, or even bliss. Within the power of its spell, nothing goes amiss. Explosive release sponsors rapid decrease in the strength of malfunctions that previously seemed to have force, before being cleansed by divorce from their source through complete intercourse with a much lighter reality. Laughter is love in its most boisterous expression. It erases all damaging transgressions. This destruction of everything negative and demeaning sends sorrow careening through darkness to meet its demise as the giggles arise.

A good laugh rips through fear and depression as fast as a knock-knock joke through a kindergarten class on the first day of school.

91

The Locks on the Doors

I like to give the Nuns and Monks their privacy. They are busy thinking important thoughts and deleting lesser ones. They don't need interruptions. Monk Mee and Monk Chaiyote live in the next two cabins up the hill from mine. In spite of wanting to leave them to their work, I go visiting now and then.

They have both been kind enough to tell me I'm welcome at any time. I am always glad to see them too. Both Monks are very enjoyable company and patient with my language handicap. They are true friends.

I went up to say hi yesterday, but neither Mee nor Chaiyote were in.

They both had padlocks on their doors.

This is very peculiar!

Minor weasel-like or drunk-punk-kid type thievery and overcharging foreigners at certain stores can happen, but blatant burglary is almost unheard of in Honoria. This is especially true in tiny rural villages such as this one where everyone knows everything about everybody. Folks know what time their neighbors get up in the morning, where they go, what they own, and a lot more. No one here could even possess an extra possession without the whole village knowing about it. There appears to be complete honesty and integrity within the community.

Jails here are brutal, but they are not the worst part of being caught for burglary or robbery. To get caught stealing from a fellow Honorian makes for a big loss of face. *Losing face* that big is a very bad thing. No one wants to know you. To lose the respect of your community is considered a fate worse than death here.

Add to this information the facts that only a drug-crazed lunatic would steal from a Monk almost anywhere in Asia, and that we live on an otherwise deserted rocky mountain with ass-kicking bears, poisonous snakes, and scorpions. Besides that, our residents have adopted poverty as a way of life and actually have nothing to steal! Locks on Monk doors are more confusing to me than the sudden appearance of a naked starlet in my bed.

In the afternoon, I tried to ask Chaiyote and Mee about the locks. Either they didn't understand my question or I didn't understand their answer. Maybe both.

As we started visiting each other more often I would sometimes walk up to their cabins with them, or leave when they left. I noticed they were staring at the locks for much longer than necessary when they opened or secured them. As they stared at the locks, their lips were moving and they had that meditation/chanting glow in their eyes.

I suddenly *got it*. The locks aren't locks to them. The locks are symbolic. When they go out, they want to remember to lock their minds against both internal and external factors that might cause imbalance. When they come home and open the locks, they are telling themselves that the Buddha (and probably whoever else can make it up that hill) is warmly and openly welcome into their home and life.

It's a great system, but there will never be a lock on my cabin door. There's something else that needs my attention. I need to trust people again. I think about that when opening and closing my unlocked door.

I visit my friends up the hill more often these days. We lock up against our worst potential and unlock our best tendencies together at the doors they've taught me how to use.

They also like walking into my unlocked cabin.

92

Jealousy

Jealousy seems to be an even more popular sport in "developing countries" than it is in our current Western civilization. In many ways, Honoria today is similar to America in the 1950s. Many of the folks here are trying to keep up with the Joneses and want to have more stuff than the next guy. People ask each other about what they have and how much it cost. Some of it is idle curiosity or just making sociable conversation, but some of it is so they can feel bigger than you or jealous of your stuff.

This accomplishes nothing. James Brown may have put it best when he sang, "The way I like it is the way it is. I've got mine, he's got his."

Whether living in the Taj Mahal or eating pizza crusts out of garbage cans, nothing that someone else owns will influence what another person has.

No one else can get poor enough to make us rich. No one else will ever get sick enough to make us healthier.

Any jealous desire, from wanting to own the neighbor's car to wishing for the guitar skills of Jimi Hendrix, is going to end in the same two truths. The first is that if we are happy with what we have then we are rich. The second is that if you want something for yourself, no amount of looking over the fence is going to get it for you.

These prove true every time.

Jealousy holds no common sense. The Nuns and Monks, being human, must have also had this little problem to deal with at some earlier point in each of their lives. Of course, having already renounced material possessions, they probably aren't coveting the neighbor's cow, fishing net, or velvet Elvis painting. The clergy all seem to be very secure in their own skins now—but they weren't born as such emotionally accomplished humans (at least not according to Western theory). It is likely that they had to work at replacing jealous notions with more productive ideas.

They seem to have figured out that *our attachment to objects of desire* is what has the real power over us. This has nothing to do with the fact that other people have stuff. It has to do with the fact that we want stuff. Leaving other people out of it simplifies the equation. The Temple residents seem to have done this. It has freed them up to go about the business of getting the stuff they want, instead of wasting time noticing what someone else has.

93

Opinion

As far as I can tell, the Monks and Nuns here don't have many opinions. They try to look at things and people as those things and people are, without attaching any subjective judgments to their observations.

I'm not very good at this yet.

Opinions are like assholes. Everybody's got one. I guess there's nothing wrong with that unless a person thinks that his or her particular opinion includes a right to impose that opinion on others.

Many folks can't find their own opinions or would rather be accepted than awake, so they borrow opinions from other places—friends, church officials, politicians, sports celebrities, parents, traditions, etc.

During the past half century I've heard a lot of opinions on every subject. Hypnotized people, unaware that they have been hypnotized, often just repeat opinions from the so-called News as if those opinions were facts. The News is a very suspect source. It is often the worst possible place to borrow an opinion.

My favorite type of opinion is called "the self-righteous bastard's opinion." The person holding this opinion thinks that God has directly and personally given him that opinion as well as the authority to throw it in your face. This person expects an "Amen!" after his opinions are voiced and gets disturbed if folks won't join him in trying to mandate his opinion into law.

Folks rarely have the courage to come up with opinions about themselves. Opinions usually come from outside sources in the first place, and more often than not they are about things external to us as well—they both come from and relate to somewhere else. That somewhere else is usually *someone* else. It appears to be only humans that have opinions at all, and the favorite subject of human opinions seems to be other humans. (The limited evidence available shows that animals and plants don't bother with opinions very much.)

The human concept of "opinion" makes sense to my occasionally cynical opinion of Homo sapiens intelligence. That opinion says that if a truly original thought ever tried to cross a human mind it would need to get thoroughly drunk in order to reach the other side.

I've traced some of my own opinions through the immediate source that I got them from, back to that source's source, and on through the swamps of time and history to the original known source of that opinion.

Interesting trip. Try it sometime.

You may find, as I did, that things are what they are in spite of what anyone's opinion says they should be. You may find, as I did, that most opinions seem to be failing attempts to bend objective reality to fit our little personal collection of perceptive mechanics, lusts, and fears. When self-centered desires and conditioned perceptions haven't much of a connection with what is objectively real, we develop an opinion to justify why or explain away why not.

I'm not sure that's OK. It sounds a little like mental illness. But that's just my opinion.

94

Things Are Fine Just the Way They Are

Things are fine just the way they are. This is true more often than not. Oddly enough, most folks don't believe it.

The Monks and Nuns, however, seem to think things are always the way they are supposed to be. They never show discomfort with the way things are. I can see their point.

Most folks get pissed off occasionally about minor things. Some folks get pissed off on a regular basis about minor things. Most of these incidents aren't important enough to waste any time or energy on, yet we allow them to be thorns in our sides. We might do better to realize life's minor mishaps are no big deal and things are fine just the way they are.

> *"It is almost impossible to overestimate*
> *the unimportance of most things."*
>
> John Logue

Sometimes a situation really sucks and it'll take a while and a lot of figuring before things are fine just the way they are (or will become). We might be better off thinking things are fine just the way they are, anyway.

Two reasons.

First of all, as Arjan is always pointing out to us here, there is some positive benefit to be gained from every experience. We just have to know how to mine it, how to dig the gold out of the dirt. Secondly, even if we can't find that benefit right away, it can still be helpful to practice having the attitude that things are fine just the way they are—*knowing* that the beneficial part of any lousy situation will eventually show up. It can, for an example, help to tell yourself that you are happy while you are still in the process of becoming happy. This is sometimes referred to as the "fake it 'til you make it" method. Others think of it as a form of bliss programming. (Still others call it bullshitting your self.)

As with so many things, the practice of *making a conscious effort to feel the truth of* "things are fine just the way they are" actually increases how often it happens that things end up being fine just the way they are! The Monks and Nuns have taken similar approaches to some far reaching intellectual and spiritual lengths, but the basics of this approach can apply to anyone and be helpful to everyone.

Finding some patience and calm will help anyone to eventually see that lesser luck is temporary. Many things that appear to be major problems may just be minor inconveniences that will eventually hold some benefit. From there, "things are fine..." can actually produce itself in emotional and physical reality!

It seems to have worked, and continues to work, for me. The more I tell myself that things are fine just the way they are, the more fine things show up. Not the least of the improvements is that many things formerly considered big troubles I now recognize as little bumps on a mostly hospitable road. Many little mishaps that used to have a damaging affect no longer have the power to mess up my day. Cappuccino, filtered cigarettes, and many other trivial habits and former addictions are no longer seen as "needs." A shaving cut or even a broken toe are not major disasters. Bad times end.

We've all heard it before, and it's still very true. What you choose to put out there is what comes back to you.

> *"You don't get what you ask for.*
> *You get what you are."*
>
> Dr. Wayne Dyer

It may be that simple.

I Get By with a Little Help from My Friends

Everyone knows the tune.

It has been a major influence on many young folks, especially those growing up in the late 1960s. The Beatles standard was an anthem to the teamwork necessary for surviving a chaotic social structure and intense personal mind expansion. It resonated with a generation that was in complete disbelief of, and disenchantment with, everything that the previous generation had handed us.

Friends on the same path meant everything to each other. We were disassembling and then reassembling reality. We were doing a lot of potentially dangerous exploration in uncharted waters and we knew it. When our individual dinghies sprung a leak and started to take on water, we were each other's life preservers.

(Brian P.) Patty Ayers was my best friend then and still is today. We met in Brooklyn when I was twelve years old. We became drug dealing partners. (See Chapter One of *Fearless Puppy on American Road* for details.)

I sent the first thirty pages of this writing to Patty and our friend Andy, asking for nothing but their thoughts and not expecting an answer. We've had little contact since I've been here.

A surprising barrage of encouraging emails followed from Andy, Patty, and several others who had been shown the material. They sent enough money for me to stay at the Temple more comfortably. I can finish writing this book here while continuing to get my feet back under me. There is also enough money to get back to America.

Remember that interesting piece earlier in this chapter about how everything changes? It's true, but some things won't change for at least a lifetime. Having friendships that last a whole lifetime is among the greatest luck anyone, anywhere can ever have.

Rambling About the Most Positive Aspects of Honorian Culture

(and more tourist information)

~ 1 ~

An old expression says, "It takes a whole village to raise a child." Every woman in this country is part of that village. I've seen mothers leave their infants in the care of teenage girls they had never met before—at bus stations. There was no doubt in that mother's mind that baby would be safe and happy when mom returned from the bathroom, telephone, or wherever she had been. Trusting strangers is more dangerous and so not as common a practice in the capitol, as would be true in any of the world's major cities. But otherwise, national solidarity, especially as it involves the care of children, is very much a part of life.

A few things account for this usually intra-family function being a national norm. A strong, broad-based national unity is partly responsible. This is a country that was never conquered and colonized by a European power. It is a lot more tribal and more homogenous than most nations.

Another aspect is the singularly maternal focus of most Honorian women, in light of the lack of equal employment opportunities. In comparison with the Western world, very few management positions in Honoria employ women. Things are changing. Modern attitudes and new technologies are gradually rooting themselves in the kingdom, but for now these are rare except in the biggest cities. Rural Honorian women traditionally learn to care for children, cook, and do household chores at a very young age. A woman may work on the staff of a vacation resort, in construction trades (often doing the heaviest manual labor!), or as a teacher, but her earliest and most pronounced education is always in childcare and homemaking. It is expected that this will be a woman's primary if not sole function in life.

Honorian folks traditionally marry very young. Mid-teen marriages are as popular here right now as they were in America a hundred years ago. Such older customs often cause friction while they rub up against rapidly modernizing attitudes. This fosters a personal-growth-versus-traditional-systems conflict that has triggered a skyrocketing divorce rate. Many single women are raising children on 100 Baht ($2.40 U.S.) a day. They do this on their own, or with the support of parents or friends who are in very similar financial and social conditions. There is a powerful, unspoken kinship among the female population here, and the children of this kingdom have a full nation of mothers to care for them.

~ 2 ~

Spirituality is accessible in Honoria. Anyone can become a temporary Monk or Nun.

In most other spiritual disciplines, including the Buddhism of many other countries, there are far more rigorous and long term commitments required for entering the program. Honorian Buddhism allows any citizen to experience devotional kindness as a way of life. These short trips to Nirvana often provide permanent benefits. We have kids at the Temple right now living as Monks-for-a-month during school vacation. They wear robes and shaved heads, just like the full timers.

When a parent or grandparent dies, a child of that family traditionally lives for a month at the Temple, praying for the departed loved one.

On the negative side, any screen whose mesh is not tightly woven can allow entrance to bigger bugs. Sometimes criminals come to Temples and become temporary Monks to evade the law, but that seems just as well. No prison in the world, much less the infamous Honorian prison system, could possibly produce the high quality rehabilitative atmosphere of a Temple. The kindness, self-control, and discipline introduced during a short stint of Temple life can be very rehabilitative for a person lacking those qualities, and for the society that will have to live with that person again soon.

~ 3 ~

If you want to get something done quickly or find something out right away (in the Western sense of those expressions), Honorian culture can be very frustrating. A large percentage of life here is devoted to fun and games. The strict businesslike efficiency and service of the western world is often looked at as manic and unnecessarily intense behavior. As Westerners, we often mistake foreign happiness and low stress levels for laziness and inefficiency. Looked at in a different light, Honorian playfulness and its refusal to allow stress-provoking situations to control life can admit us into a more peaceful way of thinking, and a pretty damn lovely way of living. Rural Honorians have a health and happiness that we Westerners have been craving since industrialization brought us into the era of high blood pressure and heart attacks.

~ 4 ~

Bigotry is the idea that one human is more or less human than another human based solely upon culture, national origin, or skin color. It is nonsense, of course. Cultural differences, on the other hand, are real. They need to be evaluated fairly and accurately in each case and respected for what they are. What I initially perceived as bigotry and racism here was often not bigotry and racism at all. It was more like a cultural difference.

This cultural difference seemed bigger and meaner to me than it was. That was partially because of my hangovers and circumstances, but not altogether. It also had something to do with how little exposure most of these folks have ever had to the rest of the world. This lack of exposure can lead to some hastily self-referenced evaluations by the natives, but these hasty judgments are usually not a personally directed attack or malicious effort to degrade. An ingrown frame of cultural self-reference is, almost by definition, a part of anything that refers to itself as a culture—especially one that has never been conquered and subjected to external influences.

After walking the proverbial mile in Honorian moccasins, I have a much greater appreciation of the goodness within the kingdom.

Getting out of the way of my own bullshit has been a wonderful thing. It has allowed me a much better and friendlier view of my neighbors.

97

Editing/Finishing

It is almost time to give this book a once over in order to make sure all the commas and periods are in the right places, and that the ideas have been clearly presented without my burning Ganja holes in reality. These finalizing processes are a lot more important than I ever figured they would be.

I've never been much of a finisher. It has always been fun to get a good idea, build on it quickly in a frenzied pitch of creativity, and then just say, "Fuck all" near the end and let it finish itself or let someone else do it.

Experience has advised me to change that approach. Letting anything or anyone else finish for me might not turn out well. If that happened, I wouldn't have a damn thing to say about it. My name is on the book. It is my responsibility to make whatever I do into the best possible finished project.

A friend of mine in the restaurant business told me, "You can serve the best meal ever cooked but if the coffee at the end sucks, that's what people will remember."

The best way of getting something done exactly the way you want it done is to do it.

In many cases that isn't just the best way—it is the only way.

98

Stoopid!

If nothing else, this story has shown that everyone can learn and that anyone can change. Any person with a brain is in charge of that brain and has both the ability and responsibility to direct where it goes. Oh sure, we are each a little different from the other. Individuals within any group are bound to be a little quicker or slower and possess different strengths and weaknesses than the others. But every one has the potential to be more like a demon or god than they already are. Anyone can spend their whole lives being painfully bounced around by uncomfortable confusion, or can learn how to reason their way to intelligent happiness.

No one ever called me the brightest bulb in the fixture or the sharpest knife in the drawer. It took thirty years for me to learn how to use chopsticks. I would have starved to death as a child in a country without forks.

Half of my first ounce of Ganja was wasted while learning how to roll a joint. That was a very long time ago. That skill has been mastered by now. My parents didn't trust me to do anything safely. I had to learn things at twenty years of age that most people got to learn at ten and perfect by twenty. After this stunted development, it took another twenty years to build the confidence to do those things comfortably and correctly. My first experience of using a power tool came at forty years of age. I'm still not good at it but at least I'm harmless. Figuring out how to put a condom on didn't happen until age fifty, but that was more about growing up in the Free Love, pre-AIDS-scare generation than it was about being too stupid to do it. In certain ways, being born a long time ago had advantages.

The crazier portion of my youth was spent shooting up intravenously—not only vast quantities of all the standard powders but Ganja tea, Jack Daniels, LSD, and other things that I won't mention here so as not to scare or repulse you further.

Yes sir and ma'am, I was scared of things that weren't there and fearless of things that everyone should be very, very scared of. In 1967, high school classmates elected me "The Person Most Likely to Die." Many of the people who did the voting are dead now.

Not a mere major leaguer, I was accomplished at all the standard minor stupidities too—putting fingers in boiling water to see if it is hot, tripping over my own feet, drinking way too much more alcohol after already drinking too much, and so on.

Big and small stupids, I've done a million of them and learned the hard way to not repeat them—by repeating them.

"I learned my lesson again."

Bryan P. Ayers

There were times I wasn't smart enough to know the difference between a light bulb and the full moon. But folks were mistaken in thinking me stupid, and I was mistaken in thinking myself stupid too.

Stupid people can't learn as much as I have.

Final Scenes

The meaning of any story depends upon the reader's interpretation as well as the author's reality. Many folks will see this story as an encouragement. Others may see it as a suggestion, a lesson, or even a warning. There will be other points of view as well.

I've tried to represent all those points of view for you here while sticking to the facts.

Endings often announce new beginnings.

This is especially true of *Reincarnation Through Common Sense*.

99

This Should Have Been the Last Chapter, But Shit Happens

The author and main character of this book is not the main character. The people surrounding him are what the book is really about. The author is a person usually steered by decent interests and intelligent trainings from wonderful teachers. The poor bastard was shocked by a long, long series of traumas. These were aggravated and intensified by massive alcohol consumption. He went wacko, but was lucky enough to land in a Temple where he received some very unusual and effective treatment. He is now enjoying a resurgence of psychological and physical health.

But the strange combination of his unusual situation today and the fifty previous years of bizarre living may be causing him some stress. His change of direction was wonderful, but not gradual. Any rapid and severe changes, even the good ones, can stress a human system. Our protagonist hasn't developed the discipline to control his own mental stability with any consistency. He often floats, as most people do, in and out of assorted states of mind without being fully awake to them.

I'm still working on the discipline and control things here and now at the Temple. It may take some time. That's fine. This is a nice place to be. I may never leave. Maybe I'm smart enough to stay. It seems a much better idea than backsliding into some less pleasant, less sane, and more dangerous place.

Staying in this Temple may even make more sense than going back to America. It certainly makes more sense than some of my other available options. Going six hours up the road to the infamous town of Hua Hin to write another book is one of those options. It would probably be titled *English Teacher in a Whorehouse*. I've been told that the many brothel owners in this town are anxious to have their girls speak English in an effort to improve customer service. English teachers are in high demand. Parts of that job would be fun but it doesn't take a psychic to know that the experience wouldn't end well.

I am honored and grateful that you have traveled with me through this whole story. I hope you enjoyed it. Thank you very much.

100

This Could Have Been the Last Chapter!

Before wrapping this up I'd like to be absolutely sure, one last time, that you understand why we have been calling Thailand by the fictitious nickname of "Honoria."

Blind anger often strikes out at anything within striking distance. Mine did for a while. I didn't scream or throw things at people, but for a short while I laid the blame for my own misfortunes on others. That was unfair to this country and everyone in it. A mind is the responsibility of its owner. Mine was more than a bit out of control and unfortunately sprayed a little venom with no regard to direction. There are variations from one place to another but people are people. There is nothing wrong with the people of Thailand that isn't just as wrong with the whole human race. Thai culture actually has several wonderful qualities that we in the West would be wise to imitate.

By now, this country feels like family to me.

I've made it my business to avoid the so-called News for the past thirty years. I don't read newspapers or watch TV reports. Yesterday I goofed by reading a whole English language newspaper. I found it on a table at the tea shop in this strange new town. The newspaper finished delivering a thought that has been on its way to me for a very long time. Three bottles of wine later, everything suddenly became clear and easy to figure out.

War has been going on forever, as has crime, greed, and all other kinds of fear-based reality and its selfishness. As Mr. Carlin said about the human race, "Humanity is circling the drain and I can't wait 'til it goes down. Every other living thing on the planet will certainly be in much better shape if the people disappear." Reading the News always proves how right Mr. Carlin was.

It also proves that being right sometimes doesn't help.

I've known this without, and before, any prompting from Uncle George. For several decades, when folks asked me where home was I would just point to the sky. Imitating a visiting alien from outer space was easier back when there was a lot of LSD around. I can remember telling people, "I'm no part of this nasty show. You are all fucking nuts! People are constantly killing each other to gain shit they don't need. The whole operation is built from our own choices and we choose to live in a violent cesspool." It seemed best to detach from earthly bullshit by continuing to play the ET card.

All the great freedom and justice movements throughout history have habitually ended in retrogression back to the bullshit that spawned them.

In the newspaper today there was an article about peaceful protestors being arrested in America. The protestors don't want their tax dollars spent on their government's paranoid plans to commit deadly mayhem. The powers-that-be want to bomb nonmilitary, civilian targets in a nation that contains more illiterate shepherds than dangerous weapons—and they want to use their own citizens' money to sponsor the bombing.

Many of our government's plans seem to include more than righteous indignation, more than just dispensing justice to parties deemed responsible for atrocities. It seems to include our own versions of atrocity. It seems to include haphazardly murdering innocent bystanders—farmers, mothers, children, pets, and wildlife. The purpose of all this misguided mayhem seems to be the reaping of profits for assorted corporate-industrial vipers that already have more money than could be spent in fifty lifetimes. This is all done behind the disguise of "national security."

It will surely result in a severe and lasting effect that is the opposite of national security. Many forms of national insecurity will result from these malicious reactions that are based upon greed and fear, and not at all upon a sound security system or a practical sense of justice.

This movie is a sad and poorly produced rerun for most of us. America has been involved in, if not initiated, at least one major war for every twenty years of its history. We have all been around long enough to see a previous version of the war we are watching now.

None of them, with the possible exceptions of the two World Wars, have been essential.

Truly brave American nonviolent protestors involved in a very real battle for freedom will continue to be thrown in cages. Truly courageous and well intended soldiers will continue to be involved in misinformed efforts to reap profits for the rich, often at the expense of these soldiers' lives and always at the expense of the innocence that told them they were fighting for the freedom and safety of their loved ones. Many realize a very disturbing fact by the time they come home—if they live to come home. They realize that the war their government and culture had led them to believe was an idealistic war was actually an economic one.

All wars are a three-foot-thick brick wall of economics painted with a veneer coat of idealism in order to attract participants.

Nonviolent protests yield results slowly. Meanwhile, the beat goes on. You can bet that by the time this book is published, many baffled foreign children and their gun-toting parents will have been buried under bomb-induced rubble that used to be their homes. Many dead American soldiers will join them in whatever oblivion wasted lives inhabit. Even easier money is a bet that when the action is finished in the country where it is now taking place, "The War" will show up elsewhere. The responsible parties never really end war; they just move it to a new country. In the case of our modern made-for-TV wars, "set" is probably a more accurate term than "country."

Multi-topical insults of humanity are just too easy after reading a newspaper, so I'll try to stick to the war angle here.

I'm not going to get sidetracked into talking about the cigarette industry. Everyone knows that it has always been a murder-for-money business that thrives on the slavery of its labor and clientele alike.

It would likewise be too easy to get sidetracked by the continuous stream of environmental disasters. The poisoning of earth, air, and water in the name of profit and progress has been responsible for the deaths of millions of humans, and a countless number of the Earth's other former species. This is also common knowledge.

Everyone already knows about the Drug Cartels (pharmaceutical companies) and their medical industry pushers who prescribe drugs that they would never take themselves. If a pill relieves asthma symptoms but produces a fatal heart attack, this is not a good trade-off.

We are also aware of enough facts, even if we are not courageous enough to be outraged by them, regarding the efforts of the weapons-and-war industries.

We know all these things, but no one does anything about them.

We have had a few true leaders. They informed and guided us honestly with real dedication and empathy.

They always seemed to get killed off by the assholes.

In the grade schools of America during much of the 1950s and 1960s, sirens would regularly send children scurrying to dive under their desks. This drill was a preparation for when the Russians would drop the atomic bomb on us. By diving under our desks, we would be protected from the flying glass of shattering windows when the attack happened.

Years later, a few former military executives with a stroke of conscience admitted that the Russians of that era *never* had the capability to land a nuclear device in America. The whole fear-based scenario was bullshit. That's not the part that amazes me. The truly baffling part of the theatrical production known as The Cold War was the part about the flying glass from shattered windows. The fear was so imbedded in people that they only thought about what they were told to think about. No one considered the absurdity of the flying glass scare.

What about the atomic radiation? If they dropped the A-bomb, what would be the point of diving under your desk? Is it important to avoid cutting your finger on window shrapnel while you and your sneakers melt into the same pile of goo?

American media is now telling folks to put duct tape and plastic over their windows for protection against impending germ warfare attacks by Middle Eastern extremists. People have a much bigger chance of dying from the fumes that will be produced by the incineration and inhalation of the plastic and tape after this scripted and dramatized hoax-to-produce-fear is exposed for what it is.

Fear produces human sheep. Sheeple do as they're told. They follow. They don't ask questions. They pay blindly for protection.

"People who would sacrifice freedom
for security deserve neither."

Benjamin Franklin

Folks are again busy believing the same kind of bullshit that they have fallen victim to for generations. The hollow threats of minimal enemies are once again the scapegoat. They hide the greed and ulterior motives that decay our nation, world, and individual lives from the inside out.

Why can't we remember that it wasn't true last time?

I don't want to hang out with people any more.

I've seen a lot of goodness in a lot of folks. I'm happy and calm now. I love all the people in this book, and (although you might think I have candy for brains to say so) I actually love everyone.

I feel a little off balance right now. Things aren't making much sense again. But I know what I have to do.

With no doubt and in every case, I recommend that you do something else. Y'all are Earthlings and you have your lives, your children, and their children to protect. I'm a tired-ass visitor from another planet who's been literally dying to go home for a long time now.

I wish I could have been more help to people while I was here. Maybe we will meet again in newer bodies but right now I need to go home.

I wish you well.

Goodbye.

[EDITOR'S NOTE: Douglas (Ten) Rose was found dead on April 4 in a hotel room in Hua Hin, Thailand. The coroner's inquest listed cause of death as a combined alcohol and drug overdose. There was no note. We can assume this book was it. The only other writing in the room was a big "MLK" in marking pen on the mirror. His friends suggest that Ten timed his death to coordinate with the assassination day of one of his heroes—the late Reverend Dr. Martin Luther King, Jr.]

101

The Answer to the Question "Why Be Vigilant?"

Sorry about that last bit. You knew it was a bad dream, didn't you? I hope it didn't bother you as much as it bothered me.

Of course it didn't really happen.

I rarely drink anymore, but did get pretty buzzed with Mr. Noi one night last week. Being already drunk didn't stop me from bringing an additional full bottle of wine back to my guest room.

Next morning, the previous chapter and an empty bottle were on the desk. I don't remember writing the chapter or drinking the wine. It feels like I had no more to do with those pages than the plastic part of the pen did. The chapter seems to have written itself.

It is ugly. I want to delete it but the message is too clear and too important to ignore. Those pages conjure up a frightening specter in a book that has otherwise tried to kick fear's ass throughout. It reminds me of just how essential it is to keep consistently in touch with oneself, to be vigilantly aware of what direction the mind is taking, and to keep building interior happiness up to a strength so complete that no external circumstance can bend it.

Happily-ever-after endings are built of daily practices. *Every* day needs to be intentionally steered toward being a happily-ever-after day. No days can be taken for granted. A period of not paying attention can result in a horrifying reality. Horrifying realities often appear to arrive suddenly, but the evidence usually shows otherwise. The evidence of most major episodes shows pressure building over time before actual blowups take place. The daily practice of exercising mental stability reduces the possibility of blowups.

I have learned over the past few months not to let external negatives throw me off center. (Although three fuggin bottles of wine can throw almost anyone off center!) The legacy left us by Barbarous Bin Laden, Brutal Bush, Satanic Sadam, and the soul-less Wall Street institutions very much responsible for the collapse of life-as-we-used-to-know-it couldn't even spoil my day. It certainly can't damage my attitude enough for me to terminate my own survival.

Being human is generally a good thing. I like to think that I'm human enough to hang tough with my peeps, to help repair societal damage, and to work toward preventing any future damage that brutal, mindless folks might like to cause.

Dying for a cause usually puts an end to what you can do for it. Living for that cause can accomplish almost anything, and perhaps everything.

VIGILANCE—THE BIG BRAIN VERSION

Here is what I have learned about vigilance through the example and silent instruction of the people around me.

When things feel right, when life's sweet and tight, it is probably due to continuing vigilance. A mind that is fully awake won't allow good intentions to break. Everyone knows that what we pay attention to grows.

"What you appreciate, appreciates."

Lynn Twist

Paying attention to living well will cause the swell of success and happiness. Not paying attention will yield the opposite. There is no good time to rest on laurels, or get too celebratory or lazy just because you find yourself in an agreeable place. It could be easy to wind up backwards again by losing attention to the wise interventions that turned things around for the better in the first place.

A long period of feeling good but not paying quality attention to what we are feeling good about can allow random joys to swallow attentiveness. At that point we can produce a mess that can cause a regress back into distress.

The antidote is vigilance.

The mental maintenance work still needs to be done no matter how good things are going. Nothing is worse than stagnation that's growing. Neil Young was correct. "Rust never sleeps."

This problem is remedied by paying attention to how we arrive at the places we thrive and then continuing to expand on what got us there. Consistent vigilance keeps the good stuff on line. It rejects bad tendencies. It keeps our best instincts refined in the mind.

Too much self-satisfaction can lead to careless infractions of allowing lesser thoughts to set in our minds. To avoid this, *insist* that thoughts be the productive kind.

In relationships the basics are consideration and response ability. A lack of these can produce the kiss of death for any relationship—taking the other person for granted.

On the more personal front (relations with self) it is almost the same, but an internal game.

If lack of attention allows unexamined decisions by rote, if we're blindly consumed by a happiness bloat that makes us ignore what has kept life afloat all along, you can bet your sarong that things will go wrong before too long. There is always the danger that lethargy, complacency, and negligence can set in. That's when vulnerability to internal as well as external nonsense begins.

Standing comfortable guard on thoughts is like fixing a car—to replace broken parts we must know what they are. The answers sought are most readily brought by non-thought. It clears the mind. A clear mind makes it easier to find solutions to the pollutions that make us distraught.

Thought needs to be addressed constructively. A relaxed consistency dissolves malignancy from the mind, making space for ideas of a more functional kind. Vigilance gives minimal attention to bullshit and does not attach to it. We cannot deny emotion but can watch, cut and paste, and delete at will when appropriate. One's own mind is the only part of the universe that can be completely under one's own control. It is a simple matter of adjusting thought to where you want it to be. It is an acquired-over-time skill like playing guitar or shooting pool in the bar. It can be that easy.

It's like walking *somewhere*, not just walking around.
First things have to come first.
Feet must be on the ground.
The preliminaries must be sound.

You have to know where you want to go and have the courage to begin the trip. You have to know that it's a bad idea to be watching, much less producing, soap operas on your cell phone while crossing a heavily trafficked street. You have to know that it is a good idea to look both ways, no matter how confident you are or how easy you think getting across that street will be.

"Watchfulness is the path to immortality
and thoughtless the path to death.
The watchful do not die,
but the thoughtless are already like the dead."

The Dhammapada

"The type of motivation that we need for doing our daily practice
is the same unchanging one that we have for getting up each morning.
We need the same intentions and determinations that we have for
going to work to earn our daily living and pay our bills."

Lama Karma Rinchen

P.S. Like everything else, this is harder for a person who has worn himself thin. It takes stamina to progress and strength to begin. A balance needs to be struck between work and rest in order to secure your vigilance best. The better you take care of yourself, the more wonders can be accessed from your shelf.

It is much smarter to take a convenient nap at home than to need one in heavy traffic!

102

We Move On

One of the greatest teachers I have ever known is moving the classroom.

The few rich businessmen that control the Temple/Village Area Committee think the Temple is not "developing" quickly enough. Their definition of development has to do with construction of new buildings. Arjan's definition of development has more to do with promoting spiritual progress and caring for needy people in the village.

The few committee big shots, coincidentally owners of province-wide construction companies, make policy for the vast majority. Although that majority is often in complete disagreement with them, the policies of the committee hold sway by virtue of the power given to the committee by the majority.

(Why does this sound both crazy and familiar?)

Arjan would rather use Temple funds to get the lady with polio a wheelchair, buy food and medicine for the poor, sponsor books and tutoring for the illiterate, or provide a new life for the family that lost everything in a fire. The committee would like Arjan to spend more money and time on construction than on his community's needs. They would also like him to temper his functional heart-based approach to spiritual leadership with more traditional fundamentalism. They would like to see more concretizing of religious symbols as well as more concrete being poured.

The committee seems content to satisfy itself while the Buddha and what he was trying to tell us get left out on the road to starve in the heat. Neither the Buddha nor Arjan can feel lonely on this account. Many great women and men throughout history have been out on that same road.

There is more of a problem here than just construction-lust and materialism. Arjan does things differently. That difference makes the traditionalists nervous. The committee thinks it most important to present a conservative image and *prosper*. Arjan thinks it is more important to actually do some good in the world. "Good" looks fine on paper to the committee— but they don't want it interfering with their bottom line.

Arjan will not back down or be forced into violating his devotion. The committee gave him an ultimatum to steer the Temple's activities in an inferior direction and left him no options. At least a few Asians have learned quite a bit from watching our American Mafia movies.

Arjan quit his position as the village's spiritual leader this morning, after the second very loud meeting with the committee in as many days. Most of the Temple residents are leaving as well. They are leaving in support of their teacher, and in the knowledge that each might better serve his or her purpose by packing all best intentions off to other locations.

We will all go our separate ways. Logic makes it seem unlikely that I will ever see any of these people again.

Where will I go? I have no answer to that question. Life will be getting very interesting in just a few minutes.

Wherever I end up, it is Arjan's kindness and wisdom that helped me live long enough to get there.

Arjan said something on our way out that struck me deeply. If there is such a thing as reincarnation into a new body, I will remember Arjan's words for a thousand lifetimes. *"I am from this place and you are from halfway around the world. From the very beginnings of our lives we have eaten different food, worn different clothing, and embraced different customs. We have thought different thoughts and performed different acts, but still—we are friends. Don't ever forget that."*

I won't, Master Teacher. I won't.

103

The Future Calls — Nine Natural Gifts

We all went to a neighboring Temple to collect our thoughts. Arjan advised us to carefully consider options before moving further on. The Head Monk at the neighboring Temple told us that we were welcome to stay for as long as that planning might take.

The Monks and Nuns carry only one extra robe, some undies, a toothbrush, razor, and a string of beads. There wasn't even time to unpack those. Two hours after our arrival at the neighboring Temple, we received the following information from our village.

One of the very few wealthy members of the community, who is not a member of the Committee, loves what Arjan has done as a spiritual and community leader. This man has just given Arjan rights to an incredible fifty acre piece of land.

Our Master Teacher will start a new Temple just seventeen miles from the old one. He has been kind enough to invite me to join his extended family and take part in the effort.

I continue to be a very lucky man.

I have offered to write and sell books in the West to help sponsor the new facilities. It seems like such a good idea! Maybe I'll sell a million and extend the effort to help sponsor Tibetan Monks and Nuns, Native American Shamanic people, and other Wisdom Professionals worldwide. That ought to keep me out of trouble for a while.

We have developed a plan for much more than a Temple. We will have a self-sustaining community, not dependent on or motivated by anything but a conviction to improve the quality of life on Earth for as many living creatures as possible—without imposing any bullshit on anyone or accepting any. It will provide a very rare public access to authentic Honorian life and to at least some of the amazing benefits that Wisdom Professionals offer.

The plan is to build an education center and vacation resort next to the new Temple. The money raised from people staying in its guesthouse and using the facilities can fund the needs of new Monks and Nuns as well as the needs of current ones.

The visiting world community can make its own schedule. Guests will be free to take advantage of the educational opportunities, to have fun, see the sights, or do nothing at all. The choice is always up to the guest—lie in a hammock, Buddhist teachings, tours to the beach or Honorian night life, yoga, massage, art and cooking classes on premises, swim in the river, gaze at the mountains, study, play, work, party, whatever.

The following travel advertisement will be sent around the world when we are ready to open.

THE NINE NATURAL GIFTS
RETREAT AND EDUCATIONAL RESORT

Secluded mountains are minutes from the ocean.
Plantation and jungle offer breathtaking views
in a safe, friendly, peaceful village.
See the real Southeast Asian native life.

Reasonable rates. (We're not here for the money.)

Choose from bungalows with comforts, tent camping,
or hostel style dormitory accommodations.

There is a grocery store.
Kitchen facilities are available
for those who like to cook for themselves.

River on the premises has pooled areas for swimming
in clean, refreshing, mountain stream water.

Enjoy inexpensive and delicious native food
at our on-site restaurant.

Produce used in our restaurant and store is
organically grown on the grounds and includes a
pick-and-eat-as-much-as-you-like natural fruit buffet.
This features our plantation of rambutan, mangosteen,
pineapple, coconut, jackfruit, durian,
and other delicious local favorites.

Meat, fish, and vegetarian dishes are all available at the restaurant.

ༀ

Beautiful waterfall is accessible by jogging and bike paths.
Bicycles provided.

ༀ

We can arrange tours of local culinary, historical, religious, cultural,
and natural interest sights, entertainment venues, or a ride to the beach.

ༀ

"Arjan," Master Teacher and Head Monk of the Temple
at the far end of the grounds, may be available
for classes in Buddhist theory and meditation,
depending on his other obligations.

One hour meditation sessions are held at the Temple each evening.
The public is welcomed to participate or observe.

Please respect the privacy of the Monks and Nuns
within the Temple compound at other times.
They visit the resort section regularly.
They love to practice English
and other languages with visiting guests.
See them there.

❧

A semi-professional American author and self-proclaimed hitchhiking dog
will be working with local teachers in native Honorian and English
language camps, classes, and private lessons.

❧

At the farthest end of the property from the Temple
(known as "The Brooklyn Acre"),
the language teacher is also the manager
of a small place of entertainment and alcohol
that features music from the other side of the world.
He has an advanced degree in culture shock
and teaches an occasional class
(more often an ongoing free seminar at the bar)
on local culture and customs.

Regularly scheduled group classes with professional
teachers include native cooking, yoga, and massage.
Classes are also available by appointment for individuals.

❧

Traditional health massage therapists always on duty.

❧

Experience the authentic
and enlightened culture
of this tropical paradise.
Our setting is one that tourists
are rarely privileged to
anywhere in the world.

You are always very welcome.

104

Just Make Yourself Comfortable

During my first month at the Temple I was constantly asking Arjan, "What can I do here?" I didn't ask out of boredom or a feeling of obligation, but out of a real desire to do something useful. It is always nice to feel useful.

Arjan's consistent answer to my "What can I do...?" question let me know there was no sense in asking any more. Waiting for a functional response like "Clean this" or "Paint that" proved to be a dead end every time. His answer without exception was "Make yourself comfortable."

I didn't get it, at first. For me, "comfortable" would have been any opportunity to be helpful and busy.

Eventually, it seemed best to give up looking for a chore and take Arjan's statement at face (sur-face, as it turned out) value.

With the level of understanding I had at the time, the main emphasis of his answer seemed to be on the word "comfortable." So I relaxed, started worrying less about being helpful or busy, began swimming in the ocean, reading, writing, meditating, and hanging out with the Monks and Nuns more often.

After a while, everything around me seemed more agreeable. The language barrier eased a little and the heat seemed less oppressive. All the wild strangeness subsided and life seemed more friendly and less threatening. Everything around me truly became more comfortable to be with.

That's when the big *SNAP* happened in my brain. The realization rattled me.

It finally became clear that by being more comfortable as a self and more comfortable with the process of living in my own skin, I had automatically become more comfortable around others and more comfortable for others to be around. The emphasis of Arjan's answer had never been on the word "comfortable," but had always been on the word "self." "Make your *self* comfortable."

Nothing around me has changed during the several months since my psychotic arrival at the Temple. Everything is exactly the same as it has always been—same ocean, same people, same everything. Nothing external has gotten more comfortable to be with.

I have.
My attitude is the only thing that has changed.

I don't have to ask Arjan how to be helpful around the Temple anymore. My Self is now comfortable enough to spontaneously and intuitively come up with answers to those questions, and a few others.

"I have lived on the lip of insanity,
wanting to know reasons
and always knocking at the door.
The door opens and I find that
I have been knocking from the inside."

Rumi

105

Would You Rather Be a Finger
or Part of a Hand?

Waiting for God or Congress to fix things won't work. The Collective Human Attitude cannot change until the attitudes of the individuals composing it do. This has been proven many times. Great Masters have come and gone. We remember their words and immortalize their faces, but the practical applications that were the truth of their teachings have been as consistently mislaid as a teardrop in the rain.

Why?

It may be true that some people are just too fucking lazy to change their minds. The bigger problem is that many of us are too stressed out, distracted, and preoccupied to concentrate on the process of making this a truly better life for our selves and a better world for everyone. Inhumane stress levels numb us into surviving under comfortably fossilized lies instead of living with truths that might be disturbing in the very short run, but will save us in the long run.

The inhumane stress levels that modern people suffer are largely fueled by two pieces of drastic misinformation. Nearly all of us have been brutally misled regarding the qualities defining our most critical human directions—*the purpose of life* and *the meaning of success.*

Repaired working definitions of these terms are necessary in order for us to produce peace and decency on an individual level. Only after plenty of that has been accomplished can peace and decency arrive and survive at the national and planetary levels.

The bigger masterpiece can only be painted by the combined brush strokes of all our little self-portraits.

All the great teachers, religions, and spiritual traditions seem to be pretty unanimous in their on-paper notions of the terms *purpose of life* and *success.* The purpose of a human life is to achieve health and happiness, and to assist whatever else is alive to do the same. The meaning of personal success is in developing the individual decency and courage to promote that universal well being, and in building the skillful means to turn that brilliant motivation into something realistically helpful to self and others.

No *One* can save us now. Salvation has been circling the planet for a long time. It can't do much without a place to land! We have to provide that landing pad by personally moving toward what we are asking for, by becoming peace and cooperation, and by leaving a lot of old bullshit behind.

It can be difficult for a person to independently redirect his or her focus. Millennia of now outdated conditioning and our present-day hypnosis by modern media only scratch the surface of what needs to be overcome.

But we have to start somewhere.

The best place to start may be to simply make our selves comfortable.

There are very few insurmountable obstacles in life. What may seem like insurmountable obstacles at first are more often just severe challenges. Most of us can victoriously rise above any challenge presented by making a comfortable but determined effort to do so. This holds true whether that challenge comes from the most evil corner of the world or the darkest corners of our own minds.

"There are no problems. Only solutions."

John Lennon

Appendix 1

Why the Monks and Nuns Are Who They Are 3

Why is this here instead of being in Section Three along with Parts 1 & 2 of "Why the Monks and Nuns Are Who They Are"? There is a good reason for that and an even better reason why this material is included at all.

Reincarnation Through Common Sense is from start to finish a true story. I want to give you as realistic a picture as printed word can carry. Some of the specifics in this section apply more to the Tibetan style of Buddhism than they do to the Southeast Asian style. It would not have been altogether true and accurate to put this within the story that is the first part of this book. That's why it is back here in its own Appendix.

106

The Basics of Protection, Mental Stability, and Happiness Through Mantra Recitation — As Seen By a Puppy

For all the differences between schools and sects of Buddhism, the basic ideas are very similar. The motivation is always a good one, the goal is always to end suffering in oneself and others, and the function is always to be as decent and compassionate as humanly possible. The following information explains elements that apply to all types of Buddhism, even if some processes are more Tibetan-specific. This information may not be directly tied to this book's story in everyday physical terms, but is certainly tied to the story at a much more important level.

"Mantras" are phrases/prayers/aspirations that are a sort of mission statement. They encourage a person to identify with the good attributes that the mantra mentions. They work to familiarize the mind with what that mind wants to become.

If any idea is continuously repeated in the mind, the person who is focusing on that idea will eventually absorb the qualities that it represents. Try putting a smile on your face and repeating "I'm happy" a few hundred times. You will be happier when you are done than you were before you started. On the other side of the coin, try watching the same TV program or commercial a thousand times—especially if it uses dizzying pace, shock, violence, fear, coercion, and various other subethical marketing techniques. Even if that commercial is selling something you wouldn't ordinarily buy, you may soon find yourself a few dollars lighter with a belly or garage full of crap you don't need.

A mantra is often repeated with the fingering of each bead as a person works his or her way around the hundred and eight bead rosary. Buddhists call the rosary a "mala." Many faiths throughout history have also used rosary beads to count repetitions and focus concentration. These beads are helpful but not essential to practicing mantra.

There are many different mantras used within Buddhism. Each is usually associated with a deity. Deity means something different in Asian schools of thought than it does in Western religions. Asian deities are symbolic, archetypal representations of qualities and states of mind that we humans strive to increase within ourselves (as well as being reference points to more cosmic possibilities).

Deities are projections of psychological powers that are within each individual person. They are also cosmic, but their real place is within.

The most internationally recognized Buddhist mantra is probably "Om Mani Padme Hum," the phrase relative to the Tibetan Deity of Compassion. There are many reasons for its popularity. One of them is the popularity and desperation of the Tibetan cause. The Dalai Lama and many Tibetans of similar spiritual brilliance have developed a lot of international support during the past fifty years. Everyone from Harvard to the 'hood has become familiar with at least a bit of Tibetan culture.

Another reason for the international popularity of this deity's mantra is that everyone benefits from an increase in compassion and the wisdom it sponsors. But the main reason for the overwhelming popularity of this mantra is that all religious and spiritual systems worldwide are based on compassion, love, and kindness. This universal theme crosses all cultural boundaries and strikes a common chord with the main teachings of all the gods and prophets of every era and location. Without compassion, the mind is like mud. It is cloudy, and its true clear nature is hidden. Compassion makes understanding your mind much easier.

Many pictures and statues of the Tibetan deity of compassion somewhat resemble a human. Many other deities in Tibet and throughout Asia are much more unusual in physical form. There are, just to mention a few, a blue half-man/half-bird deity, a four armed crimson female deity with a bow and arrow, and a giant ferocious black creature about as large as the smiling, fat buddha seen in American Chinese restaurants.

When people repeat the phrases associated with these deities and picture their images, it isn't for the purpose of asking, nor do many expect, a giant blue half-man/half-bird (just for an example) to come out of the heavens to give them protection, happiness, and mental stability. The purpose of repeating the mantra phrase over and over again is to absorb the positive qualities associated with that mantra, *to become it*. One works to absorb, embody, and manifest the qualities represented by the deity. In that way we become the power that is being invoked. Many Nuns and Monks put a lot of work into raising positive qualities within themselves by reciting mantras.

The half-man/half-bird symbol representing protection may be commonly accepted as a fairy tale, but the cumulative effect of internally repeating the mantra message of protection *does* train your mind to be vigilant against its own mismanagements and to recognize external obstacles before they become a danger. It is a very real and empowering process.

We become what we pay attention to. Focus on happiness, mental stability, and protection deeply enough and you will be happier, more stable, and more protected. When you become and own the qualities of the symbolic "god" or "goddess," you will protect your thoughts as they arise. You will steer them toward being the best human thoughts they can be. This will often account for better decisions regarding your protection, happiness, and stability in the external world. Again, thoughts that are in conjunction with the deity representing them instill deified qualities in the human who is thinking them.

The world often cooperates with a benevolent point of view. Folks who associate themselves with the beneficial qualities represented by deities are happier and less afraid than most people. Such people are often concerned with the well being of others. Their own problems are lightweight.

Strengthened thought patterns will develop through the mental exercise. The consistent repetition of positive concepts can strengthen the mind just as efficiently as pushups can strengthen your arms.

Eventually, a person will become very keenly aware of the qualities he or she is trying to metabolize. This increase in awareness translates rapidly into the ability to avoid external as well as internal stumbling blocks. You will look both ways before crossing the street and when you do, you will see more in that same space than you ever did before. You will, whether consciously or subconsciously, set up the circumstances that will arrange the conditions that will engender the causes that will keep you and whomever you point good thought at happier, more stable, and more protected in various internal and external ways.

This is a real life functional scientific system, folks, and there are a lot of symbolic deities to choose from in order to reinforce any number of good qualities.

All these deities offer different roads to the same metaphysical place— that of being a distribution center, no matter how large or small, for universal altruism. This spiritual generosity is not related to sappy romanticism, dysfunctional addiction, or a suffocating attachment. This unbiased love, compassion, and generosity are practical applications of a human decency that may be the necessary missing ingredient to insure our survival.

A standard and very important point of procedure in Tibetan practices is to dedicate all time spent on this personal god-becoming (absorbing the positive qualities of the representative deity through mantra recitation) to the benefit of *all* living things. This dedicating is usually done at the end of the meditative session but many think it important to keep this point in mind during every single recitation of the mantra phrase. This reminds the practitioner that the effort is not just for little-brained selfish purposes. In effect, you are sending positive qualities out to the Universe with every mantra repetition, just as surely as you are absorbing them.

Unfortunately, a human mind is also capable of sending and absorbing anger, hatred, and stupidity. But human decency and compassion are so built into these practices that the system contains an automatic failsafe device. Karma is that failsafe device. *Woe be to whoever would try to use any parts of this system for selfish gain at the expense of others.* There's something you won't do twice! Ouch! Besides the pain that will be involved, you are guaranteed to not achieve your desired result. The old "you reap what you sow" expression holds very true here.

As good qualities are practiced and thought about, they grow and become magnetic. As you internalize qualities of compassion and protection in your mind, there will be more compassionate and protective circumstances, people, and things drawn to you. Like attracts like. As you practice giving it away, it comes back to you. Karma never fails here either! Whether a person's actions are nice or nasty, he or she will always, in some form or another, eventually get a return in kind on their emotional investment. You don't have to be religious to know that what goes around comes around. Most Agnostics and Atheists also know this to be a fact of life. Physics majors know it too. Every action has an equal and opposite reaction.

The proper spiritual mechanics in use of these mantras is essential. This is another good reason why all these practices are best done with the guidance of an educated, experienced, patient teacher who is very familiar with these processes.

The more we think of happy, strengthening, positive things, the more firmly that becomes the ground state, the normal condition, of our mind. Much of what Monks and Nuns do involves methods of programming themselves with repetitive thoughts of bliss and compassion. Similar practices in other, non-Buddhist spiritual traditions have been referred to as *Bliss Programming.* It works in more ways than you might expect. It works in more ways than we can even imagine. The process of continuously, repetitively focusing on something that becomes an integral part of your character can be as essential and basic as potty training. It can also be as dangerous as intimidating news programs, exaggerated advertising, and propaganda—or as constructive as bliss programming and mantras.

Once you do a lot of this repeating, and picturing, and absorbing, and becoming of a mantra/deity, you could say that your brain's receiver is tuned to that frequency. Much like a radio, the mind/brain picks up and interacts with what it is tuned to. A chef is more likely to know where to find that ingredient the stew is missing than a guy who has hasn't touched a stove since he moved one into his house. In the same way, a dedicated mantra practitioner would be more skillful at finding safe and peaceful solutions to problems than the average person. This is true whether those problems are between people or within that one person.

When you get so well tuned to the qualities of a deity that you have metabolized them and have actually become the embodiment of those qualities, something strange and wonderful happens. There's a shift in your frame of reference. The more cosmic and esoteric information and connections can arrive at shift time and thereafter. You realize that you are not only attuned to the symbolic deity's qualities but are also on the same wavelength as others who have pictured that deity and recited that mantra—as well as all those, of any culture, who have ever mustered that deity's qualities within themselves—whether they have ever heard of that deity and mantra or not!

The Dalai Lama is Buddhist and Mother Teresa was Catholic. They were born on different sides of the world speaking different languages and with a totally different idea of what the word "deity" means, yet they have a lot more in common than most Christians do with each other or most Buddhists do with other Buddhists. They share a wavelength of decency that is far more potent than any of the differences between them. They have pictured the same essential ingredients and universal forces behind their differing symbols.

As the space between you and the deity diminishes, you may get the feeling that the space never existed. You would not be alone with that notion. That school of thought says that the practitioner and the deity are and have always been a unit, but the union was obscured by the mundane concerns that constantly run through our minds much of the time—budget, relationships, job, car, etc. These concerns need part time attention, but when given too much attention they can take up an entire life and blind us from seeing the bigger and better parts of ourselves. Michelangelo was well known for his belief that any sculpture he carved was already there within the rock. All he did, he said, was to chip away the excess.

Reciting mantras can do the same. It focuses the mind on a point, on a quality to be absorbed—a quality said to already exist within each living person. Any psychological excess housing information that is no longer useful or relevant is crowded out of existence by the more positive and useful information replacing it.

Once you get to know them better, the frightening and monstrous deities turn out to be just as compassionate as their smiling counterparts. Even the most ferocious and demonic looking deities and iconic creatures are doing such jobs as feasting on the flesh of anger and jealousy, or drinking the blood of attachment and ignorance.

Deity mantras provide transport to a bigger picture and a more inclusive frame of reference. A mindstream that causes problems, when properly nourished, repairs itself into a mindstream that can create monumental solutions. The human that has absorbed the qualities of a deity can unite with the amassed energy package that composes the metaphysical substance of that deity to produce an amazing creation. The awesome power of such a deified person's mental integrity yields a strong command over his or her own less desirable qualities. That usually results in more productive dealings with external situations. When you are master of yourself, all things fall into place and become beneficial.

Is it crazy to think that picturing a deity representative of protection and compassion while reciting repeatedly something akin to "I am protected and a compassionate protector" can draw protection and compassion into actual functional existence? Isn't a bridge, or a building, or a party, or a war just someone's mental creation—an idea, a thought that we pour power, resources, and effort into and create in the physical realm?

Don't all human accomplishments and physical constructions start as a simple thought, emotion, visualization, idea, or conviction?

I'm the wrong person to ask. There's a rumor around town that I'm crazy.

But I can tell you this. I have seen one of these amazing creations! It was a massive blue birdman that ate anger and stupidity. He protected me from both externally generated and self-inflicted bullshit. He told me that we had known each other for a very long time before we ever met.

Everyone sees through his or her own eyes. I describe things that have been triggered awake in me by severe personal circumstance and extended contact with robed people, but these are still my own perceptions. These are subjective views of personal experiences.

If you want authentic teachings, find an authentic teacher. I am not one.

I am still just an adopted dog that is writing a book on paper towels and bar napkins with a ballpoint pen found in the road.

On the other hand, there are a few things I actually do *know* to be authentic.

These deities have different characteristics, but do not have aberrant personalities. One won't get pissed off and kick your ass if you hang out with another.

The "mind" of all these symbolic deities is the same. They are various fingers on the single hand of love/kindness/compassion. The aim of each deity is to help people develop those qualities in the particular way that works best for that particular person, and eventually for that person's interaction with all living things.

❧

What we might call esoteric, mysterious, and cosmic considerations can arise from these deity practices. Every individual has his or her own depth of experience. Depth expands with time and intelligent practice. To have a mystical experience doesn't necessarily mean that the experience isn't grounded in science. It might mean that our knowledge of science is limited.

❧

These symbolic deities and the Wisdom Professionals who infuse those deities into their own lives know that there is no greater ally than a consistent focus on good intent. They know that "Pure love casts out fear," and "Nothing holds us back but what we are thinking." They also know that there is good reason why these phrases are famous to the point of being cliché.

Everyone reading those words knows that they are truer than whatever we choose to live by instead of them. The material facts may support the idea that our everyday grind is more important than those two clichés quoted above. Intelligent practice of mantras can help save us from the shortcomings of material facts. In the words of Frank Lloyd Wright, "The truth is more important than the facts."

Recognize and then make a habit out of the single mental ground where we are all united—and then hold fast there. Make this present-tense awareness the meditation. Thoughts always come and go. But the mind that these thoughts come from is more eternal than those thoughts. It never comes and goes. It is always there. Don't grab at the temporary thoughts. Don't get attached to them. Instead, be what never goes away. Be the clear mind that sees, observes, all the thoughts coming and then going. This awareness is the buddha within you. It is your real self, unclouded by reaction to either internal or external bullshit.

107

Lama Karma Rinchen

Lama Karma Rinchen is Tibetan, not Honorian, but you will see from Lama's quotes just how much the Honorian and Tibetan branches of the Buddhist tree agree on the basics. So do most Wisdom Professionals worldwide, regardless of culture or religion.

Lama Karma Rinchen escaped the Chinese occupation of Tibet in 1959, crossing the Himalayas by himself. At eighty years of age he now travels extensively, teaching in places as diverse as Asia, Hawaii, and Truth or Consequences, New Mexico.

Here are a few of Lama's words that address the ideas we have been talking about throughout the book. Like so many other genuine Wisdom Professionals, his way of saying things can contain simplicity and depth in the same sentence. I hope this authentic teacher's words give some additional clarity to whatever I may not have made clear enough.

∽

"Everybody has the same potential for spiritual growth, and that potential goes far beyond our normal human understanding."

"...We have to be able to see clearly, with no doubt about it, that it is our mind, our own situation, that has to be worked on, and not that of others. It is not easy to look closely at our own selves, but somehow it seems to be easy to look closely at the faults of others. In Tibet we have a saying that it is easy to see a flea on the nose of another, but impossible to see a yak on our own nose."

"It is our mental habits and tendencies that fuel our thoughts and actions from moment to moment. They are the cause of all that happens to us, and we need to become deeply aware of this. Underneath our habits and tendencies is pure awareness, which is our own true nature, and this is what we are looking for. It is very hard to make progress...if we have a feeling of disbelief that such an accumulation of habits and tendencies has become boss of our mind."

"Discursive thought, fueled by accumulated habits and tendencies, constantly describes what it touches. Our own true nature does not try to describe what it is aware of. It is pure, without elaboration."

"Discursive thoughts make us think we cannot exist without doing exactly what we have always been doing in our daily life."

"When a thought arises, we won't need to suppress or cut it off, which causes stress. It can just be let go. We don't have to give any attention to the thought at all."

"From then on we can develop the discipline to not follow our thoughts, and they will leave no imprint on our mind."

"Being aware of thoughts arising in the mind will give us a sense of responsibility for all of the actions we take, as well as their results."

"There is no question that it is difficult to clean and polish the mind. Our mental habits...have developed great strength and don't want to give up their power."

"There are no other methods that will bring us to the realization of full and complete enlightenment than the ones that purify the mind of all of the accumulations."

"It is not...things in themselves that are a problem, but it is the mental attachment to them that creates the difficulty."

"...if it has been a long time since we experienced compassion, then we have great difficulties in seeing the view of others."

"As we gain experience, we should not pretend that we are enlightened, or pretend that we are the least little bit superior to others."

"Accomplishing these practices is like finding that we have regularly been taking a poison, and now we have unexpectedly discovered an antidote that will cure us. The poison is what has kept our mind chained to the cycles of the relative world, and the antidote exposes us to the ultimate nature that we all have...There is a difference between the relative view and ultimate view. The closer we watch the mind, the greater the possibility there is that the awakening to the ultimate view will happen to us."

"The *Tibetan Book of the Dead* also describes visions of hell beings, hungry ghosts, god realms, and things of that nature. These visions are of our own creation, and not something that is coming at us from outside our own mind. The visions are our own habits and tendencies, and they come at us like demons. There are many methods that are there to help us recognize the illusion. The teachings say that a dream is like a small death, and death is like a big dream. If we can recognize that we are dreaming while we are actually having the dream, we can make changes in it."

"Always, whatever we do,
we should do in a gradual and steady way."

Lama Karma Rinchen

Appendix 2

Why The Dog Soldier Trilogy Is Being Written

This explains a bit about our project to sponsor Wisdom Professionals. There are a few laughs in here too! If you've read *Fearless Puppy on American Road*, you've seen this.

108

Why The Dog Soldier Trilogy Is Being Written

The Dog Soldier Trilogy is a collection of two books.

The first one was written second. The second book was written first.

There will be a third book written about what gets done with the money made from the sale of the first two books. That, of course, means that folks will have to buy the first two in order for the third one to ever come about.

The Dog Soldier Trilogy is about many things but is presented as the story of a single human being. It would also be reasonable to say that it is about all human beings. Most of us could easily relate to the main character. Many of the mistakes made by humanity as a species have been made, one at a time, by our individual hero.

He's been busy.

If fuck ups were feathers our boy would have wings. He seems to constantly bounce between extremes of disaster and bliss that rarely rest in stability. It is also true, to give credit where credit is due, that our protagonist occasionally embodies bits of what makes human beings worth the trouble it often is to deal with them.

These books read very much like novels. Many folks who have read them think that they are fiction or fantasy. They are not. Most of the content in both books is true. Some of the facts within these books may be jumbled. Details have been recalled by a memory that is suspect. By now you understand why the author's memory is suspect. What happens in real life doesn't always leave documented proof in its wake. These books are real life.

A few names have been changed to protect the privacy of my friends. Some more have been changed for my own protection, legal and otherwise. Very few names have been changed to protect the innocent. Very few people are actually innocent, especially in the first book, *Fearless Puppy on American Road.* Folks who were my hosts on the road related some of the stories in *Fearless Puppy* to me. I'm a pretty good judge of bullshit by now. If a tale appears at all, it means that I'd bet money on it being fact.

This second book, *Reincarnation Through Common Sense,* is a different story. It is also a factual account but involves more folks who could truly be called innocent. Most of this book was drafted while residing in an Asian Temple.

The stories in *Reincarnation* can be more strictly described as totally true because in this book I have personally seen everything that is described. All accounts are firsthand.

The experiences described in *The Dog Soldier Trilogy* can be considered nonfiction in *Reincarnation* and very creative nonfiction in *Fearless Puppy*, but they are nonfiction nonetheless. I know this to be true because I am the main character.

Fearless Puppy on American Road is about a teenage drug dealer in Brooklyn, New York who runs away from home to hitchhike around America for thirty five years or so. The reasons for my never learning to drive a car are well stated in the Foreword (*I'll Tell You Why*). Whether the decision to never drive was a brilliant one or illogical stupidity is debatable. That some very interesting things happened because of that decision is not.

As you know, this second book, *Reincarnation Through Common Sense*, is about my rescue and adoption by a Temple full of Monks and Nuns in Asia. I was there for almost half a year after suffering my near fatal incident. As you have seen, most of the book describes living in an atmosphere of high level common sense and spirituality, but there are a few major twists to the story. The first is that I couldn't speak the native language and no one there spoke English, so the book puts silence into words. The second is that I was in a Buddhist temple but never studied any Buddhism (certainly not in any traditional sense). The third is that most of the book was actually written as a conversation with you. I hope you agree that some very interesting things happened in this book as well.

The third book that describes what is accomplished with the money made from selling Books 1 and 2 will be called *Sharing the Bones*, or maybe *God, Dog, Kibble*, or something just as ridiculous.

Writing is fun for me. I hope this writing is also fun for you to read—but *The Dog Soldier Trilogy* has a purpose to it besides recreational entertainment. Here it is.

There doesn't seem to be any efficient political solution to the world's problems. We can elect as many different Chief Bozos as we want to but we'll still be living in a circus of suffering. As long as the thoughts, conversations, and media of humanity are focused on war, greed, drama, and problems instead of happiness, peace, and solutions, we will always be, as they say in Brooklyn, "in a world of shit."

Many of us are constantly worried that we live on a planet that wobbles dangerously out of control. Actual horrors notwithstanding, life on Earth is friendlier than we have been led to believe and can be made friendlier still. Many of us regular folks have realized this and chosen to do something about it. We have assigned to ourselves the job of getting happier. We also try to present positive, truthful information and happier options to our fellow humans. The purpose of all this is to recognize, refute, and help repair the result of the negative information and options that we have been depressed by for so long. If people have more access to happier options, ideas, and attitudes, it will be easier for us all to become happier, kinder people.

Most folks have some very good tendencies, but these tendencies are often warped by stress and misinformation. These tendencies need to be exercised and strengthened past the point where they can be compromised. We need as much reinforcement and support in doing this strengthening as we can get. We need more people who are professionals at bringing about these happy and helpful kinds of thoughts and actions in themselves and others—especially those who are so serious about it that they completely dedicate their lives to making it happen.

In present day America we are blessed to have many such folks, and they are pretty blessed themselves. Many of our professionals-of-the-positive are doing well. Deepak Chopra's sold a lot of books. Bernie Seigel, Iyanla van Zandt, Marianne Williamson, Wayne Dyer, and many of our other brightest minds live in comfortable circumstances. Oprah seems to have a few bucks left over, even after the expense of all the wonderful activity that she sponsors. That's great. These people deserve any prosperity that comes to them and more.

My point is that many of their equals in America, and especially in other parts of the world, are not doing so well. There are many forms of Native American, African, Asian, Australian, European, and other assorted wisdoms that are endangered. Those who are preserving these wisdoms within their small local cultures often lack the resources for decent survival, much less the wherewithal to make what they know available to us. I've met some of these folks. Some live in very average American towns. Some live on the other side of the world. A lot of what they know could prove essential to all of us.

Asia provides a clear example. Over there, much of the positive counterpart to greed, brutality, and ignorance arrives through the compassion and loving kindness of a school of thought (it doesn't require a religious interpretation, folks) known as Buddhism. It is the route most folks over there (and there are a lot of them) use to get back to their more humane side. When life gets harsh, if people get lost and foul, the Monks and Nuns are well equipped to direct those people to the road that leads back to a sane manner of living. They have the training, dedication, and patience to help everyday folks find their individual peace. This of course helps the society at large to stay manageable, friendly, and happy. The Monks and Nuns of Asia are the Wisdom Professionals who remind people of the human decency within and their obligation to exercise it.

Many of these professionals-of-the-positive throughout Asia lack many of life's basic necessities including food, clothing, and shelter. The resources and facilities do not exist for their numbers to expand in conjunction with modern humanity's need for these people.

As a rule, Monks and Nuns don't have paying jobs. Their survival is dependent upon the generosity and gratitude of a population that is nearly as poor as the clergy themselves.

The life of a Buddhist Monk or Nun is austere even in the best of circumstances. The training is very rigorous. They do without most of the things that you and I consider essential parts of daily life. They are involved in the singular most difficult effort on earth—deep meditation. This isn't some lala brained, half assed, 1960s flashback type of effort. The type of meditation done by Monks and Nuns requires full time mental focus. Facilitating the elimination of suffering from all living creatures and developing the skillful means to do so is the goal of that focus.

Starvation and frostbite can break anyone's concentration. Although the spiritual rewards of their training are thought to be unparalleled, the trials posed by that training can seem too overbearing to endure. For some prospective beginners, those trials may seem too overbearing to attempt.

I've been lucky enough to see firsthand the powerful effect that these Wisdom Professionals can have on individual lives. I've seen it in America, Asia, Mexico, and everywhere else I've ever been.

Let's crunch some numbers. (Again, Asia is just an example. The cost of preserving North/South American, African, Australian, European, and other assorted humans and wisdom may be slightly higher, but is certainly comparable and manageable.)

It takes one dollar a day to sponsor a Nun or Monk (food/clothing/shelter) in northern India, Mongolia, Nepal, etc. For that dollar, a Monk or Nun by virtue of their extensive training, compassion, and dedication may influence from one to several million people that day. They do go on TV and make videos sometimes.

They might influence a child to do better in school. This could result in the benefit of that child, the child's family, community, and possibly all of humanity as well. That child could grow up to invent the cure for cancer, or who knows what.

Stranger things have certainly happened.

A Wisdom Professional could catch an adolescent girl at a crossroads in her life. He or she could influence that girl to become more like Mother Teresa and less like the crack whore down the street.

You may call investing a dollar a day to this process charitable. You may take what is probably a more realistic approach and call it functional or practical. Whatever angle you take, most of us would agree that this is a well invested dollar.

These professionals-of-the-positive provide the general population an available daily dose of kindness and emotional intelligence. This dose counteracts the effects of whatever bullshit has pissed the members of that general population off that day, and often reaches further to assist with long term problems. Irate people are reminded that they can be patient, compassionate, tolerant people. People on the edge remember that the world can be a decent, friendly place and that stepping on others in order to feel in control of their own circumstance may not be the best idea.

If people in any part of the world feel more happy than hostile, then people in every part of the world are safer and more comfortable. Expanded happiness pumps up the odds for a decrease of violence and an increase in the amount of peaceful coexistence we enjoy.

It seems that the information offered by these teachers of sanity spurs us everyday folks on to a state of mind more conducive to (what could be called) spiritual growth. Everyone benefits from having another good teacher around, especially when the subject of study is how to be a happier, healthier, and less hostile human being. Again—this spiritual growth is not some surface level, bullshit do-gooder, bumper sticker type figure of speech. The type of individual spiritual growth referred to here may well be the deciding factor in facilitating our survival as a species.

So, Book 3 will be about how The Fearless Puppy Project is setting up perpetual funding operations to support those who sacrifice everything in order to help the rest of us find solutions to our problems. The base funding for this effort will be the money you and your friends spend buying Books 1 and 2.

If you find *Reincarnation through Common Sense* or *Fearless Puppy on American Road* enjoyable, please tell others. Maybe they'll buy a book too. The funding from book sales will hopefully go a long way toward increasing the number of calming, helpful, enlightened, and sanity oriented professionals we have available to us.

I love and respect my fellow humans, but we've screwed up to an embarrassing proportion in at least one regard. We're very late in providing support and sponsorship for emotional and spiritual intelligence. For whatever reasons, we have historically put faith in the need for a destructive type of knowledge. This misplaced faith has backfired. Destructive knowledge is running us over.

Constructive knowledge can save us if priorities are adjusted.

If more of the folks who are willing to dedicate their lives to the increase of such things as functional, practical happiness and general sanity get the opportunity to do so, it may be our best chance to jack up the level of the circus before the bozos blow it up.

It is, after all, our circus. For all we know, the Far Eastern theory of reincarnation notwithstanding, this may be the only circus we'll ever get to attend. Doesn't it make sense to support more competent ringmasters and management?

About the Author

Please see www.fearlesspuppy.org for more details about our project to sponsor Wisdom Professionals, TV/radio interviews, and a lot more information.

Congressional Record

United States of America

PROCEEDINGS AND DEBATES OF THE 99th CONGRESS, FIRST SESSION

Vol. 131	WASHINGTON, THURSDAY, OCTOBER 24, 1985	*No. 143*

Senate

MASSACHUSETTS FOR AFRICA MONTH

● Mr. KERRY. Mr. President, I would like to take this opportunity to draw attention to the fact that Governor Michael Dukakis of Massachusetts has proclaimed November as "Massachusetts for Africa Month." Twenty-five African countries are appealing for emergency aid to fight famine, and 150 million people are facing critical shortages of food, medical supplies, health care, and water. Through a community-wide effort Massachusetts will try to do its part to alleviate these horrible conditions.

This project was initiated by Douglas Rose, a Massachusetts youth counselor. During the month of November, merchants will donate proceeds from certain business days, while local schoolchildren, senior citizens, labor unions, colleges, religious organizations and sports teams will contribute in various ways.

Mr. President, I praise Governor Dukakis, Mr. Rose, and all those involved in this program for continuing to keep us aware of the terrible plight facing many Africans. It is this cooperation of neighbor working with neighbor for a common goal that shows true American spirit and compassion. I urge my colleagues to follow the example of Massachusetts and promote this kind of community participation in their own States.

Douglas Rose: a plan for November.

Getting organized to help Africa

By Pamela Reynolds
Contributing Reporter

He says he had never organized anything bigger than a sock drawer. But sometime last May he got an idea he just couldn't set aside. Before long, the man who had trouble matching his socks had organized a project that would eventually involve such diverse organizations as the AFL-CIO, the Massachusetts Federation of Teachers, the Celtics, and the Boy Scouts of America.

Doug Rose, a 34-year-old former juvenile counselor from Northampton, organized Massachusetts for Africa Month, a project in which individuals, businesses, and state and local organizations are encouraged to contribute to African famine relief during the month of November.

In a recent interview in Brighton, Rose, who quit his 13-year counseling career to take on fund-raising full time, said he is now broke, homeless, and "borrowed out."

The African relief plan developed during a night of drinking at a Northampton bar as Rose watched a television news magazine report about a group of New York school children contributing to African famine relief. He was impressed by their dedication. He thought if they could do it, he could do it.

AFRICA, Page 74

Getting organized to help Africa

■ AFRICA
Continued from Page 73

"A lot of people have good ideas and nothing ever gets done about them," says Rose, whose salt and pepper hair flows past his shoulders.

"People say, 'It's a good idea but I don't have any clout, I don't have any power, I don't know anybody.' I was thinking like everybody else, but then I said, 'wait a minute, this is America, you're supposed to be able to do stuff like that.' So I did."

Shortly after seeing the television report, Rose persuaded youngsters from Northampton's Tri-County Youth Program, where he was working, to organize a tag sale with the proceeds going to Africa. He also called every business, club, church, and school in the area to ask them to help in raising money for his cause.

Businesses agreed to donate five to 33 percent of one day's profits. Bar owners and musicians agreed to organize benefit shows. Schools, churches, senior citizens groups, and clubs agreed to orchestrate their own fund-raising projects in which they would donate the proceeds directly to the famine relief charity of their choice.

In the midst of his feverish activities, it occurred to Rose that it would be a good idea to have the mayor of Northampton sign a proclamation declaring a famine relief month.

He made his way to the mayor's office and persuaded city officials to designate June "Pioneer Valley for Africa Month." For every day in June, Rose ensured there would be at least one corresponding fund-raising event in the Northampton/Amherst area.

Because of the success of the lo-cal effort, Rose began to consider something more far-reaching. The next logical step: a Massachusetts for Africa month. It was then that he quit his job.

After persistent phone calls to Gov. Michael Dukakis' office, he finally received a positive response. November would be declared Massachusetts for Africa Month. The proclamation would be signed Sept. 11.

"I think they mostly did it because they were sick of hearing from me," jokes Rose.

He called friends living in Boston and in September, after borrowing $600, temporarily moved in with them. What was originally supposed to be a week's stay turned into two months.

Since September, he has spent 10 to 12 hours each day writing letters and phoning organizations and agencies asking them to contribute to an African relief agency during November.

"I go through the phone book and call everything with a 'Mass.' or 'Boston' before it," he says.

His nights are spent on the floor. With no income and no permanent home, Rose has twice been forced to panhandle and will probably do so again if Massachusetts for Africa Month is successful enough to inspire a United States for Africa Month.

So far, lack of personal income has been the only problem.

"I have no place to live and no money. But that was all true two months ago," says Rose. "Hopefully, if something comes along I can find some organization to back this."

Rose refuses to take any percentage of the proceeds for himself. "This money is supposed to be going straight to Africa," he says.

Rose grew up in Brooklyn, N.Y. Back then, he never would have guessed he would eventually be doing charity work for Africa.

"I was a juvenile delinquent," he says. "I ran away from home, overdosed on drugs. I never did anything criminal but I was kind of nuts," he says. "Being brought up in Brooklyn, it's not hard to develop a wild streak."

Working for 13 years as a juvenile counselor in such places as a maximum security unit in Worcester, a group home in San Diego, and a preschool program in Oregon, his early years as a troubled youth has, to some degree, helped him adjust to his current difficulties.

"I've lived in a stairway for three months in New York," he says. "I'd like to have a place to stay, but I can always look back and say I once lived in a stairway. A lot of things I wouldn't mind having – like a bed – but then I think about those people in Africa. I'm a lot better off."

So far Rose has gotten a total of 42 individuals and organizations to agree to fund-raising activities this November, including the Boston Fire Department, Massachusetts Bar Association, Boston Boys and Girls Clubs, and MBTA Police. Coca-Cola has agreed to air its support on commercials and the New England Patriots have agreed to publicize the effort on the home scoreboards.

"The Massachusetts Federation of Teachers supported the resolution signed by the governor, and we're hoping to go beyond that," says Kathleen Kelley, legislative representative for the Massachusetts Federation of Teachers. "It would be a shame if we let the proclamation be posted and not go on from that. I have this sense people feel somehow the famine is

over, I think we want to make children aware that this is not the case."

Each organization will send proceeds directly to the organization of its choice. Suggested organizations are USA for Africa, Oxfam America, Live Aid, and the Eritrean Relief Committee.

Because contributions will go directly to such organizations, Rose says he may never know how much money his effort has reaped.

"I'm totally detached from the proceeds," he says. "But it's got to be more than a million dollars."

Even though Rose may never know how effective his work has been, he says he has proven anyone can do anything.

"People can do stuff," he says. "They don't have to get as involved as I am ... but whatever they're doing they can put more compassion into it. It's just this is the way I chose to do it."

For more information on Massachusetts for Africa Month, call Douglas Rose at 783-9675.

Orphanage in Mexico needs help

By KATHLEEN PEASE
Gazette Staff

The man who wore a cardboard box two years ago to raise money for the homeless now is seeking $50,000 to rebuild an orphanage in Mexico.

While vacationing in Mazatlan, Mexico, in February, Douglas Rose, wandered out of the tourist section of town and wound up at an orphanage called Hogar San Pablo. Run by a Catholic priest, the rundown building is home to 50 children who share one seatless toilet, Rose said.

The dwelling was a convent before it was destroyed by a cyclone, said Rose, 36. The priest and some neighbors patched it together and the priest now lives there with the orphans.

"The neighbors are poor, too," Rose said. "There's only so much they can do. And this isn't the worst place either."

The priest manages to feed the children with leftovers from nearby hotels.

Rose, who says he can't mind his own business, was already scheming during the airplane ride back to United States. His plan, according to a letter distributed to prospective donors is to raise $50,000, put it in a Mexican bank, and with the 12½ percent interest earned, generate $6,250 a month. Most would be used to hire Mexican plumbers and carpenters to rebuild the orphanage.

"It's a perpetual fund — this money will never run out. It will

live on the interest," Rose figures.

His idea, "will provide employment for local people and boost the economy," he said. "I'm definitely going back there. If you want it done you've got to go do it."

As an incentive to gain large donations, Rose said that 15 percent of the interest earned would go toward maintaining a vacation residence in Mazatlan on the Pacific coast. Rose said that could be used by people who give at least $1,000 to his project.

Rose said that in Mexico, "There are a lot of people with not such a good attitude towards Americans." He hopes to change that attitude. When he's done with the first orphanage, he plans to find another.

Raising money for various causes is not new to Rose. In 1985, he organized "Massachusetts for Africa Month" which raised $1 million to help famine victims in Africa, according to his estimate.

A year later, he wore a large cardboard box and walked from the streets of Northampton to Boston to call attention to the plight of America's homeless.

"That wasn't pretty," he recalled, "but it was like a day at the Hilton compared to what's going on down there (in Mexico). You'd have to see it to believe it."

He now heads a non-profit organization, the Legion of Volunteer Enterprises Corp. (LOVE), which lists Gov. Michael S. Dukakis among its honorary directors.

DOUGLAS ROSE wants to raise money to rebuild an orphanage in Mexico.

Rose remains homeless by choice. He stays with friends in Goshen, Holyoke, Vermont and with his father in New York City.

"I'm not hurting, I get enough to eat," he said.

Between projects, Rose works part time for Greenpeace, a non-profit environmental organization that seeks to protect endangered species.

"I like the work the group gets

done. A lot of my ideas — including walking around in a cardboard box — had a lot of Greenpeace inspiration," he said.

"The day after I get $50,000, I'm going back," Rose says with conviction. "By now I've got the reputation that the money gets to where it's going."

Contributions may be sent to the Legion of Volunteer Enterprises, 313 River St., Conway, 01341.

COMMENDATION

WHEREAS: sticking one's neck out for the Common Good is an inspiration to all;

WHEREAS: such Risk-taking is vital to a compassionate, peaceful and just world;

WHEREAS: The Giraffe Project is commissioned to seek out such Risk-takers and to honor them for their deeds;

THE GIRAFFE PROJECT
herewith declares

Doug Rose

TO BE A GIRAFFE

whose courageous actions illumine all our lives
making manifest the Truth
that people who believe in themselves and care for others
can meet any challenge life presents.

Given this 1st day of December, 1988

——————————
President

Box-dweller on statewide trek to publicize plight of homeless

By MARCIA BLOMBERG
Hampshire bureau chief

NORTHAMPTON — Doug Rose quit his job last year to raise money for the starving in Africa, and now is living in a cardboard box and planning to walk across the state to raise money to ease the plight of the hungry and the homeless.

Rose, a Northampton resident who organized Massachusetts for Africa Month in November, said recently he has been living on the streets of Boston for about a month and plans to continue living that way until he starts his fund-raising walk Sept. 1.

"It's gruesome. I ran into a guy who hadn't eaten in three days, and this is America," Rose said.

"Everybody thinks it's something they can ignore, but they don't realize the crime rate goes up in direct proportion to the poverty rate," he added.

"I'm sleeping on the streets to get the lowdown on the situation, but also to dramatize that the situation is worse than it's been in 50 years," he added.

"When the government is not doing enough, it's up to the people," he said.

Rose, 35, estimated that Massachusetts for Africa Month, which received the support of Gov. Michael S. Dukakis, raised about $1 million for starving people in Africa, but he noted that he set it up so that donations were sent directly to the helping agencies, rather than to him.

Maureen Koopman, a fund-raiser with Oxfam America, said recently that a plethora of fund-raising events for the starving in Africa were held about that time around the country and it is impossible to tell how much money was generated by the activities Rose coordinated.

She said such special events are a help, especially when they get many people involved.

Rose hopes to organize a similar Massachusetts Hungry and Homeless Month next spring, but he said he needs money to do the organizing work and his cross-state walk is designed to raise that money.

He estimated the cost of running an office, paying the telephone bill and postage costs for encouraging donations for the hungry and homeless would be about $50,000, and that is what he hopes to raise from the walk next month.

He has formed a non-profit charitable organization called LOVE, which stands for Legion of Volunteer Enterprises Corp., with himself as executive director and Dukakis as an honorary director.

A spokesman in the governor's Office of Community Affairs said Dukakis knows about Rose's work and has lent his name to the corporation.

The corporation is registered as a non-profit institution with the secretary of state's office, a spokeswoman said.

As Rose walks across the state, he will be wearing a cardboard box that he jokingly calls his house.

The former paper towel box, with armholes cut out, is decorated with brickwork drawn in ink and the words: "Thousands don't have homes this good. Join us in Massachusetts Hungry and Homeless Month."

Since Rose quit his job last year as a juvenile counselor for the Tri-County Youth program here, he has lived on the generosity of his friends and family, he said, but he needs a place to live with a telephone to do the hours of organizing work necessary to mobilize millions of dollars in donations for emergency shelters, food banks and survival centers across the state.

Robert Winston, director of Tri-County Youth, said the program "is proud that someone who worked here is working for the goals expressed by the agency, and I wish him well."

Rose is seeking pledges for his 250-mile walk, which will wind from Boston to Worcester, Springfield, Greenfield and Williamstown.

Pledges-per-mile or contributions may be mailed to LOVE, 313 River St., Conway, MA 01341.

Photo by Wesley Bilss

Doug Rose, whose cardboard box is his home, pauses on Main Street in Greenfield yesterday during his statewide campaign to raise money for the homeless.

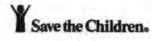

54 Wilton Road
P.O. Box 950
Westport, CT 06881 USA
(203) 226-7272

It was with great pleasure that I heard of Doug Rose's undertaking. It is an exciting concept and I am delighted with your participation in the project.

On behalf of Save the Children and the children who will be benefiting from your generosity, I send thanks.

If I may be of any assistance to you, please don't hesitate to contact me.

Sincerely,

Nanci Michaels
Coordinator of Volunteers

NM/mua

G R E E N P E A C E

1611 Connecticut Ave. N.W., Washington D.C. 20009 • TEL. (202) 462-1177 • TLX 89-2359

```
                                    Kevin Jones
                                    KEVIN'S GAZPACHO
                                    Box 263A
                                    Barr Hill Rd.
                                    Huntington, MA
                                              01050

                                    413-667-5246
```

To Whom It May Concern,

    Douglas Rose has been an employee of Greenpeace since
July 1984. It was my pleasure to have been the director
of a fundraising office of Greenpeace during a period which
Doug was employed there. Much of the experience I, myself,
gained at Greenpeace greatly assists me today in my current
natural foods business. For much of this I have to thank
the person who assisted me in many aspects of my job, as
well as doing his own - that person being Doug Rose.

    As my employee, I found Doug to be possessed of boundless
energy. When he transferred to our Amherst Mass. office
he was working as a juvenile counselor in the mornings and
a Greenpeace fundraiser (among our best) in the afternoons.
During this same period in his "spare time" he organized
the entire "five college area" of Western Mass. to participate
in a famine relief project that included politicians, musicians,
businesses, nightclubs, schools, media, troubled youth,
etc. etc. All, including Doug himself, were working on a
non-paid volunteer basis. His continuing efforts were lauded
by both senators, the governor of Massachusetts, the media,
Giraffe organizations and many others. Certain fundraising
systems he introduced to the area (business day % contributions, etc) are still being sucessfully implemented by
other local charitable groups.

    Besides being innovative and cooperative; a teamplayer
as well as a self starter, he has influenced others to channel
compassion into constructive effort and can be a powerful
motivator. People have been moved to action simply by his
unassuming example.

    I must say as well that Doug is not your simple, naive
"goody two shoes" type. His formative years were spent on
some of the meaner streets of New York City. This has given
him exceptional street smarts and experience which have
allowed him to successfully functionalize a love of things
good in a manner which may have had other well intentioned
but less clever people look foolish. He has an ability to
work within an established system while not compromising
his principles, which has endeared him to the most radical
and conservative of his peers.

BOSTON, CHICAGO, HONOLULU, JACKSONVILLE BEACH, SAN FRANCISCO, SEATTLE

286

G R E E N P E A C E

1011 Connecticut Ave. N.W., Washington D.C. 20009 • TEL (202) 462-1177 • TLX 89-2359

Peers would be his word for everybody. In my role as his director I have met very few people who are his peers.

I wholeheartedly give my unqualified recommendation of Doug Rose for any position or challenge he chooses to accept. He was my best employee and remains a valued friend.

Should you require more information please feel free to contact me during business hours at the above address.

Sincerly,

Kevin Jones
    Former Director of the
    N.Y.C. Greenpeace Office

BOSTON, CHICAGO, HONOLULU, JACKSONVILLE BEACH, SAN FRANCISCO, SEATTLE

Made in the USA
Charleston, SC
27 September 2013